Mrs Ward

Biographical sketch of S. Thomas of Canterbury

Mrs Ward

Biographical sketch of S. Thomas of Canterbury

ISBN/EAN: 9783741178580

Manufactured in Europe, USA, Canada, Australia, Japa

Cover: Foto ©Andreas Hilbeck / pixelio.de

Manufactured and distributed by brebook publishing software (www.brebook.com)

Mrs Ward

Biographical sketch of S. Thomas of Canterbury

BIOGRAPHICAL SKETCH

OF

S. THOMAS OF CANTERBURY

BY

MRS. WARD,

AUTHOR OF "GOSPEL STORIES," "STORIES FROM THE OLD TESTAMENT," ETC.

LONDON: BURNS AND OATES.

1880.

PREFACE.

IN times when, like the present, all long-established institutions are being threatened, and political order and government is assailed to its overthrow, that which is the foundation of all order, peace, and regularity,—the Catholic Church—is the first point of attack. If she can be overcome and laid low, then anarchy and confusion must prevail over all nations, and the victory of evil will be complete. Naturally, therefore, those heroes of the Church who have maintained her rights through persecution and exile, and shed their blood finally in the defence of those rights, are objects of the special hatred of all those who may be called the infidels and revolutionists of Europe. Men who would take the governance of the world into their own hands, and under the cry of liberty and equality would drive out all the institutions of God and set up their own idols in their place; such men would fain,—like our Henry VIII. when he wanted to force his own power and a religion of his own construction, of which he should be head, down the throats of the people,—cite again into Court the bones of S. Thomas à Beckett, and judge and condemn him afresh for daring by his life and his death to oppose their views. We will not stain our pages with the blasphemies they have uttered, and, no doubt, will continue to utter, against one of the greatest of the Saints of God, but it seems a time when any devout clients of S. Thomas must desire to do what little honour lies in their poor power to this great servant of God, to compensate for these insults, and to put forward the events of his life and martyrdom in order to draw attention to the firm stand made by Christ's Confessors against the spirit of evil and confusion and "wickedness in high places": that spirit which has always warred against the Church, and now walks through the nations with louder voice and tread than it has yet dared to do.

It is not the intention of the writer of these pages to enter into the arena of argument which has lately been waged concerning the character of S. Thomas of Canterbury or to do battle in his behalf, which would be alike a path to which the author is unused, and would interfere with the object of the work. The present sketch originally appeared as two articles in the "Dublin Review." They were written from a feeling of deep devotion for a Saint whose chivalrous and heroic qualities, generous devotion, and tender, yet saintly affection to his friends, and even to the base master who had once called him his friend, could not but excite the admiration, love, and reverence of those who studied his history. And it is under the same feeling that they are now republished.

Saint Thomas, like his successor in later ages, S. Edmund of Canterbury, was remarkable for the numerous miracles which succeeded his death: and the natural qualities of the Saint seemed to come out peculiarly in those miracles. At one time we read of a poor man who had aided the Saint when the latter was a poor priest, sick at the house of a friend, and who appeals to S. Thomas as a personal friend not to forget his services, but to raise his daughter to life: as though certain that the warm heart and generous spirit which had · in life never forgotten a kindness, and knew so well how to feel for those in sorrow, would not fail to come to his assistance at the throne of grace. Nor was he mistaken, for the young girl, whose body was already cold and stiff in death, raised her hand and came to life, and the dreadful disease of which she had died left her. This miracle was attested by the Bishop of Norwich and many witnesses. The arm of S. Thomas's friend, Edward Grim, also, severed by the assassins as he held it up in the martyr's defence, seemed incurable by the doctors for nearly a year, when one night S. Thomas appeared to him, and wrapping a cloth, wet with holy water and the martyr's blood, round the arm, said to him, "Go, you are healed": which was indeed the case, for Grim wrote the account with the very arm which had been disabled. Edward Grim adds, "And God has done many other things to prove His love for our Blessed Martyr: by cleansing the lepers, as we have ourselves seen; by putting devils to flight; by healing the dropsical, the paralytic, the deaf, the dumb, the blind, the lame, and those suffering from all manner of sickness; in all of which things we are awaiting the faithful testimony of the Church of Canterbury, in whose sight and knowledge all these things are known to have been done."*

After the murder of the Archbishop had been accomplished, the monks, having with

* Canon Morris's "Life of S. Thomas à Beckett," page 367.

haste closed the doors of the Cathedral, buried their martyred Primate in the crypt. This was chosen as the most secure place; for the impious family of De Broc had threatened to carry away the Saint's body by force.

No Mass was said in Canterbury Cathedral for nearly a year after the dreadful sacrilege had been committed. The Cathedral remained in mourning and widowhood, as it were; the altars were stripped and the crucifixes veiled as in Passiontide, until the Church was reconciled by the Bishops of Exeter and Lichfield by the powers sent them from the Pope, through Cardinals Theodwine and Albert.

Pope Alexander III. lost no time in proceeding to the Canonization of the Saint who had been so zealous in defence of the Church and the rights of the See of

S. Peter, and when this had been done, the Pope, writing to the Chapter of Canterbury, bids them on some fitting day, with a solemn procession and concourse of clergy and people, place the relics of the martyr on the altar or in some fitting shrine, "and try to gain by pious prayers his patronage with God for the salvation of the faithful, and the peace of the Universal Church."

This was the origin of the " Translation of the relics of S. Thomas," a Feast which is kept on the 7th of July; a Tuesday having been carefully selected, we are told by Cardinal Langton, in whose Arch-Episcopate the translation took place, as the day of the week on which the Saint was martyred. The translation did not take place for some fifty years after our Saint's death.

In 1174 the Choir of Canterbury Cathedral was burnt, but it was at once rebuilt with greater splendour than before, and the part of the cathedral where the martyrdom took place was enlarged. The column against which the Saint had stood was removed and an altar erected, on which the two fragments of De Brito's sword were preserved. The Chapel was called "The Martyrdom," and the Altar "The Sword's-point."

The length of time which elapsed between the Canonization of S. Thomas and the translation of his relics to what all devout Christians then hoped would be their last earthly resting-place, seems to have been caused by the great desire to build a chapel and shrine fitting for so great a Saint. The spot in the cathedral selected for the shrine was the Chapel of the Blessed Trinity, where S. Thomas had said his first Mass, and where he frequently celebrated both before and after his exile. It was here also that he used to come to pray and assist at the hours in choir. This chapel was destroyed to make way for the splendid shrine to which the Saint's relics were conveyed. The translation took place in 1220, and Cardinal Stephen Langton, Archbishop of Canterbury, spared neither expense nor pains to celebrate the function with worthy magnificence.

Not only the young king of England, Henry III., with Pandulf, the Legate, was present, but the Archbishop of Rheims, nearly all the bishops of the realm and many from France, as well as the Abbots, Priors, Earls, and Barons, besides the clergy and people. It was said that so great a concourse of people had never before been collected in England in one spot. That the Cardinal Archbishop was munificent in his endeavours to give honour to the day may be imagined when we read, that besides the sumptuous entertainment made in his palace, he provided at his own cost forage for the horses of all those who came to the solemnity on the road between London and Canterbury, and caused conduits to run with wine in several parts of the city. The day chosen by the Church for the translation being nearly at Midsummer, seems to have been selected from a tender consideration for the many pilgrims who would wish to attend one of the Saint's Feasts, and to whom travelling in midwinter, when the Feast of the martyrdom occurs, would be fraught with great difficulties and hardships. Pope Honorius III. granted an indulgence of forty days to all who should be present at the Translation or within the Octave; and in inviting all the faithful to attend in proper dispositions he said, "The Heavenly King, the Lord of Angels, has honoured in our time the realm of England more highly than others, and He has adorned the English nation with an especial prerogative; for while the world is in wickedness and the malice of men increasing, He has chosen from thence for Himself a man without spot, who priest-like, not only in a time of wrath was made reconciliation, but when invited to the heavenly banquet merited to taste that passion which the Lord drank. Let then the happy Church of Canterbury sing to the Lord a new song, the Church whose altar the martyr Thomas has purpled with his precious blood."*

* "Life and Martyrdom of S. Thomas of Canterbury," by Canon Morris.

BIOGRAPHICAL SKETCH

OF

S. THOMAS OF CANTERBURY.

AMONG the English Saints, there is none that has shone with a brighter light on the page of history than S. Thomas of Canterbury; and this is the more remarkable, as the portion of his life which has entitled him to a place in the Calendar of the Saints was comparatively short. Ever of spotless purity and deep and sincere devotion, the splendour and heroic daring of that great and noble soul seem yet to have been, if we may say so, at least to a certain extent, wasted upon the things of earth for many years of his life; for he had numbered no less than forty-four of them when he was appointed to the see of Canterbury. The elevation of soul was indeed there, the realization of things magnificent, glorious, and beautiful, existed and found their expression in a retinue and paraphernalia more splendid than any which had ever graced a minister of the kings of England—one might say of Europe—during the middle ages. But the glory of the king's daughter is within, and it was not meant that a mind so capable of true greatness should waste its light on the gaudy toys of earth.

Much has been said and argued by historians respecting the real character of S. Thomas of Canterbury, and of the apparent change which took place in that character after he exchanged the mace of Chancellor for the pastoral staff of archbishop. We are not disposed to contend with Protestant historians on this subject: if it is difficult for an ordinary Catholic, as it surely is, though surrounded with all the light of God's Church, and the blessings of her guidance and teaching, to enter into the views and fathom the mind, to sound the depths, as it were, of those great souls whom God has called "to shine as the stars" as His Saints—how impossible must it be for those who know not the most elementary truths from which that sanctity takes its rise, to comprehend a course of life and action which has its life-springs from those truths and that teaching which emanates from that Church, whence alone flow the waters of salvation and sanctity. Yet to show that in proportion as a "dim light began to steal over souls whom it has pleased God in later years to draw towards some vague knowledge of the truth of His Church," they began to have a conviction of the manner in which His saints have been misunderstood and misrepresented, we may make a quotation on this subject from Mr. Hurrell Froude, whose great genius never had its scope, and whose yearnings after the light of truth were never permitted to be fulfilled in this life :—

> It appears to him (the writer of this history of the contest between Thomas à Becket and Henry II.) that Thomas à Becket during the time of his chancellorship, though necessarily engaged in pursuits inconsistent with the sacred office of deacon, and though entering into those pursuits with perhaps more than necessary keenness, preserved nevertheless throughout an innocence and even austerity of character, which in a layman would have been justly regarded as a proof of unusual seriousness. This appears not only from the general assertions of all contemporary historians, who though they have shown no desire to conceal the failings of this part of his life, are yet unanimous in their testimony to this effect, but is likewise corroborated by circumstantial statements to which of course more weight is due.

The story which follows in Mr. Froude's

S. Thomas of Canterbury.

work is mentioned by several of the biographers of S. Thomas; of how one of his hosts, desirous of ascertaining by personal observation how far the Chancellor deserved the reputation he bore for regularity and uprightness of life, entered his bedroom at night with a lantern. The bed was not occupied by the great minister of state, who was however perceived by his astonished host in a profound sleep, stretched at length on the bare boards. Mr. Froude proceeds:—

Now it is obvious to say that this anecdote proves nothing; yet the considerate reader will doubtless bear in mind that it is not every Chancellor of whom such anecdotes have been preserved; nor will he regard the person of whose private habits we have this slender notice exactly in the same light as if we knew nothing of them. This anecdote is recorded by William of Canterbury, one of the authors of the Quadrilogue. From another of his biographers we hear . . . of the severe penitential discipline to which he was in the habit of subjecting himself, and adds the circumstance that when in London he received it at the hands of

Raoul, prior of Trinity, and when in Canterbury from Thomas, a priest of S. Martin's. And again, when asserting the spotless purity of the Chancellor's moral conduct, he appeals to the declaration of his confessor, Robert, canon of Merton, "from whom," says he, " I heard it myself." . . . If we could forget the fact that Thomas à Becket, when Chancellor of England, was not a layman, there are perhaps few characters of his age that we should contemplate with more unmixed pleasure and admiration. As principal law officer of the kingdom, the difficult task devolved on him of re-establishing order and good government in a country habituated to anarchy for twenty years. And the ease and rapidity with which he accomplished it is just matter of wonder. As a military commander, though without any advantages of birth, and in an age when perhaps aristocratic prejudices were just at the highest, he seems to have been the acknowledged leader of the chivalry of England. Seven hundred knights of distinguished prowess enlisted under his banner; and some of the haughtiest barons of the realm were proud to be designated his liegemen. As a diplomatist he acquired such an influence over the king and nobility of France, that notwithstanding the losses he had occasioned them in the field, and the concessions he had extorted from them by negotiation, he was received in that country with open arms, and provided with an asylum at the king's expense during the six years of his proscription. In short, there seems to have been a sort of fascination about him which triumphed alike over the interests and prejudices of all he came into contact with. His person is said to have been pre-eminently beautiful; his manners grave or playful as occasion required; every detail of his establishment to have indicated at once his splendour and good taste. Among other things it is mentioned of his band of music that it was the admiration of both armies, the French and the English. And yet this was the person who could choose bare boards for the place of his repose, and submit to the discipline of the scourge from his religious advisers. England must have retrograded sadly if such characters were ever common in her annals.

Thus far Mr. Froude. But let us go to more Catholic sources to hear the circumstances of the birth and early life of one who was to prove so great a saint and champion of the Church of God.

In Canon Morris's Life of S. Thomas à Becket, a work which cannot be too highly praised for its full and accurate details, and the deep interest of its many and varied anecdotes of the Saint, we read that S. Thomas was the son of Gilbert and Matilda Becket, citizens of London. Such is the Saint's own simple account of his parents, who would seem however to have been in good, if not affluent circumstances, from the fact of their having been able to give their son a good education. Nor were there wanting the usual wonders which mostly surround God's Saints from their cradle, and even forestall their birth.

Previous to his birth (says Canon Morris) his mother dreamed that the river Thames flowed into her bosom. Startled by so unusual a dream, she went to consult a learned religious, who, having forewarned her that dreams were not to be attended to, nor a woman's visions made much of, told her that in Scripture water signified people, but that he could not undertake to interpret her vision. She dreamt again that when she was visiting Canterbury Cathedral to pray there, the child prevented her entrance.

As the time of his birth drew near, it seemed to his mother as if twelve stars of unusual brilliancy had fallen into her lap. It is also said that she dreamt that she was bearing Canterbury Cathedral, and that when the Saint was born, the nurse, as she held him, exclaimed, "I have an archbishop in my arms."

He was born on Tuesday, December 21st, 1117, and after Vespers on the same day he was baptized by the name of S. Thomas the Apostle, whose festival it was. It would seem that S. Thomas had the blessing, vouchsafed so often by God to those whom He designs to serve Him at the altar, of a good and pious mother, who early taught him a tender love of Our Blessed Lady and a great compassion for the poor.

The well-known story of S. Thomas's Eastern origin must not here be omitted, for though there does not appear to be any deep historical foundation for its facts, it seems almost of too remarkable a character to be a mere fiction, and the fire of our Saint's temperament, and his varied and unusual natural gifts, might well lead one to suppose that he united the Oriental and Norman races in his blood.

When his father, Gilbert, was a young man, he took upon him our Lord's cross, and set out for the Holy Land, accompanied by a faithful servant named Richard. On their road, however, they fell into the hands of the Saracens, and became the slaves of a certain infidel chief named Amurath, with whom, however, Gilbert got into such favour as to be employed to wait at his table, and even to converse with his master, to whom he not only detailed the manners and customs of the countries of the West, but spoke of his religion with all the fervour of one who had braved so much for its sake. These conversations made a deep impression on the only daughter of Amurath, and yet more so, when she found, upon questioning Gilbert further, that he expressed his willingness to die for the faith he professed. The Eastern maiden was so struck with a religion which exercised such an influence over its disciple, and with the earnest and devoted character of the disciple himself, that she offered to become a Christian if Gilbert would promise by his faith to make her his wife. Gilbert, however, fearful of some treachery, treated her with doubt and deliberation, and found means, with other his fellow captives, to effect his escape; but the devotion of the Eastern maiden was no ways destroyed by his flight, and with the knowledge of only two words of English, Gilbert and London, the name of her lover, and his place of abode, to aid her in her search, she resolved to brave all dangers to find Becket. The legend tells us that joining a band of returning pilgrims, she reached London, and there she wandered through the streets, calling constantly upon him whom she sought by his name, gazed at by the passers-by in her foreign dress as if a distracted creature. Gilbert's servant Richard saw and recognized her as she passed his master's house, and told Gilbert of the strange news. Becket, with the prudence which he showed in the first instance, and which certainly seems to have outweighed his vanity, desired his servant to conduct the Saracen maiden to the house of a widowed neighbour until he could take ghostly counsel about her; then, repairing to S. Paul's, he asked the advice of the Bishop of London, and by the counsel of that prelate the maiden was duly instructed in the Christian faith, and became the wife of Gilbert Becket. Nor had he cause to repent of his marriage, for the qualities possessed by his convert wife, and which showed a heart capable of such high resolve and endurance of hardships for an earthly love, grew and spread into the highest Christian virtues, so that when almost immediately after their marriage Gilbert was seized with a pious longing to visit the Holy Land a second time, his wife urged him to give place to any plans he might form for the greater glory of God, professing her firm faith in the protection of Him who had so wonderfully hitherto preserved her and brought her into His Church, and to the perfect knowledge of Himself. Gilbert, therefore, went again to Palestine, and during his absence S. Thomas was born, whom he found on his return a beautiful, intelligent child of three years and a half old, and the admiration of all who knew him.

But we will proceed with the more strictly historical details of the Saint.

At an early age he was placed under the care of Robert, Prior of Merton, who was ever his faithful friend and spiritual guide, his confessor while he was Chancellor, and at his side when he was martyred. The earlier years of our Saint were thus passed in study, and his education probably finished at Paris, whither he seems to have gone after his father's death. By the time S. Thomas entered upon life, as it is called, both his parents were dead. His mother, whose loss S. Thomas felt very deeply, died when he was only twenty-one, and his father shortly afterwards. He went then to live with a relation who was a rich merchant, and in his house he learned much of those business-like habits which he ultimately used to the benefit of State and Church. He soon, however, passed into the service of Theobald, Archbishop of Canterbury, and there it was that his rare talents and remarkable character, which in his embassies to Rome and elsewhere on the part of the archbishop had already much advanced King Henry's interests, so drew the attention and regard of that monarch that he made him Chancellor, and entrusted him with the most important affairs of his kingdom, and not satisfied with heaping upon him all the honours and preferment which fell within his grasp, he made him tutor to his son, the young Prince Henry.

The devotion and energy of S. Thomas's character was now drawn out in the service of an earthly master, and he distinguished himself as a soldier no less than as a statesman—nor can we be surprised, considering the manners of the age, that a man who, though in holy orders, was not a priest, should, as Chancellor of the kingdom, and the king's chief minister, lead his forces to the battle-field. Lingard tells us that during S. Thomas's campaign in the duchy of Toulouse, which Henry was endeavouring to possess himself of, he took three castles hitherto deemed impregnable, and tilted with a French knight whose horse he bore off as the honourable proof of his victory. During this same campaign he brought with him a body of 700 knights at his own expense, whom he headed himself, and was foremost in every enterprise. But it was in a very different battle-field that God intended his servant should wage war; he was to contend with that very master he was now so zealous to serve, to fight for a heavenly master against an earthly one, for the interests and defence of the Church against the world, and that evil one who makes common cause with the world.

Henry the Second, to whom power and dominion was the chief aim of existence, seeing in S. Thomas à Becket a man of unbounded abilities, and a resolution which equalled them, and knowing his great attachment and loyalty to himself, proposed to himself to make him Archbishop of Canterbury, by which step he considered that he could obtain, as he wished, an entire power over the Church as over the State, and render the former his complete slave both in rights and in revenues. With this view, and with that despotic absoluteness which was a part of his character, Henry forced upon the unwilling acceptance of his chancellor the Archbishopric of Canterbury, and thenceforward Thomas à Becket was a changed man. A changed man, yet not a different man, but the character went through that sort of change which would come over a mind, vigorous, earnest, deep, and thoughtful, when it feels that the hand of God has come upon it almost against its will, and drawing aside the curtain of earthly vanities, displays by some great turn in its life, to the gaze of the stricken soul, the solemn and awful realities of the unseen world.

Something of this seemed to come as a warning voice to S. Thomas's heart when the first rumours of his probable ecclesiastical elevation reached him; for when the Prior of Leicester, who was joking him on the gaiety of his attire as being unfit for a churchman, alluded to the common rumour of his being raised to the primacy, he said: "I know three poor priests in England, any one of whom I had rather see promoted to the archbishopric than myself, for I know my lord the king so intimately that I am sure I should have to choose between his favour and that of Almighty God if I were appointed."

No doubt the years he had spent in a Court, and above all such a one as Henry the Second's, had not been without their due effect on such a mind as his, and he had been able to weigh in their fullest balance the uncertain favour of man and the short-lived glories of this earth. Once the earthly representative of an undying King, all the trappings of the worldly glory for which he had been so noted were laid aside, and the strict sobriety of the ecclesiastical "cappa" took the place of the gorgeous robes for which he had been so remarkable. Just as a seed buried in the earth springs forth into beauty and fragrance of which the mind has no conception until the change takes place, so the ideas of earthly glory being buried in the love of God, took deep root and sprang up to bloom, and finally to blossom with the scarlet flowers of martyrdom.

It matters but little to that God to whom a thousand years are but as one day, whether the period be early or late that a man masters the idea of sanctity. He looks to the *heart*, and if that is true, simple, and fervent, ready to give Him all, and adhere to Him with an unswerving devotion,—it is not for us to say wherefore He calls some of His greatest servants in the middle or even the later years of their life; why He strikes them down like the great Saint of Manresa while fighting for earthly glory, or pours the dew of heavenly tears upon them at their consecration rather than give them their fullest measure of Divine grace in their childhood or at their baptism. Suffice it that He deals differently with His Children, illustrating thus the parable of those who have worked in His vineyard in the morning, the noon, or the evening of the day.

And now that S. Thomas has thrown his whole soul into the cause of Heaven, we see the rain of Divine grace beginning to water the fields of a mind possessing so strong an impress of its Creator. How rapidly this takes place, those pious souls can best tell us who having given themselves with a strong and earnest will entirely to God, begin to feel a new life and existence in prayer and the presence of God, the very idea of which was unknown to them before. And as the storm of persecution gathered round S. Thomas, his heart deepened and strengthened in God's love. And the clouds were indeed collecting fast.

S. Thomas having been previously ordained priest, was consecrated bishop on the octave of Pentecost, Trinity Sunday, June 3rd, 1162, in his metropolitan church, by Henry of Blois, Bishop of Winchester, brother of the late King Stephen, and a man of great piety and holiness of life, whose views were raised to the clear light of heavenly truths, as is well proved by the speech he made immediately after the consecration of S. Thomas, whom he addressed thus:—

"Dearest brother, I give you now the choice of two things; beyond a doubt you must lose the favour of the earthly or of the heavenly King."

The words would seem to have been almost prophetical; and the Saint replied to them with fervour and floods of tears as he knelt for the bishop's blessing: "By God's help and strength I now make my choice, and never for the love and favour of an earthly king will I forego the grace of the King of Heaven."

The monastery of Christ Church, Canterbury was at that time under the immediate rule of the archbishop, who was its head or abbot, though the prior managed the internal government of the community, and the realization that he was in some sense a religious must have added a yet greater solemnity to an earnest mind like that of S. Thomas to the dignity of the Primacy. Notwithstanding his varied avocations, and the press of business which now came upon him, he led the life of a true monk, with such additions as his own saintliness suggested. He rose to matins with the community, after which he washed and kissed the feet of thirteen poor men, giving them a meal with his own hand; then after a short time given to repose he went to the study of the Holy Scriptures, after which he either said Mass himself or assisted at it, abstaining at times from offering up the Holy Sacrifice through reverence and humility. "Those who frequently assisted at his Mass," says his chaplain and intimate friend, Herbert de Boscham, "can bear witness to the tears and sighs the presence of his Lord drew from him, and to the very great devotion with which he celebrated." "When he was alone," says another of his intimate friends, "he shed tears in wonderful abundance; and when he stood at the altar he seemed in very presence of the flesh to see the Passion of the Lord. He handled the Divine Sacraments with great reverence, so that his very handling of them strengthened the faith and fervour of those who witnessed it."

It would appear from different circumstances in his life to which his friends and biographers allude, that the archbishop's bodily temperament and constitution sympathized with his mind, and was of a very sensitive character. He felt cold acutely, and was subject to an illness which excitement or anxiety would readily bring on, causing acute pain in his side. This explains the quantity of clothing he was wont to wear, and, added to the habits of his life at Court for so many years, would render it difficult for him to adopt all the austerity of food which he evidently desired, since not only do his biographers speak much of his temperance at table as archbishop, but in his exile at Pontigni he much injured his health by attempting to follow the rule of the monks of that monastery. And to such a temperament as we have described, delicate and sensitive both by nature and bringing up, it must have been no ordinary bodily austerity to put on a hair shirt, which is described as one of unusual severity, and which he wore from the day of his consecration till his martyrdom. His biographer, Herbert, gives testimony of his remarkable temperance at table, rendered the more striking by the need his many years passed in the world had brought of his food not being of a coarser sort than he had been accustomed to, and relates an anecdote of a person who was dining with him, and who remarked with a smile on the delicacy of his food. S. Thomas gave him the indirect advice of correcting himself before he looked about for his neighbour's shortcomings. "Certes, brother, if I am not mistaken, you take your bean with greater eagerness than I the pheasant before me."* Herbert adds

* Of such things, however, says Herbert, S. Thomas

that the reproof was deserved. "This person lived with us for a while," he says, "and though he did not care for delicacies, for he was not used to them, he was truly a glutton of grosser food."

From some cause, however, the archbishop did not leave off the magnificence of his attire till the close of the first year of his consecration; and the great sincerity and humility of his character would lead one to believe that this arose from a wish to conceal the graces which the Holy Spirit was working within. However, it scandalized the community of monks over whom he now presided; and one of the religious, "who was more intimate with him than the others,

eat very sparingly, and while he would taste the wine that was set before him and the dishes that were brought to table, his principal food was bread, and his usual drink was water in which fennel had been boiled.

reproved him for it, and undertook to relate to him a dream that one of the community had had regarding it. "Go tell *the Chancellor*," a grave and venerable personage had seemed to say to him, by the title he made use of marking his indignation, "to change his dress without delay; and if he refuse to do so, I will oppose him all the days of his life." To the reproof, S. Thomas made no reply, but he burst into tears. However, he thenceforth laid aside his gorgeous dress, and clad himself as a very priest.

His alms were abundant and profuse, and his love and personal tenderness towards the poor is proved by their enthusiasm for him as he came out of the Council at Northampton, when the crowds of poor on their knees begging his blessing would hardly let him pass; and on his return to England, after his exile, as will be seen as we pursue his life to its close.

Following out the scheme of absolute power which Henry the Second proposed to himself, this king no sooner saw his former Chancellor in the right position, as he considered, to subject the Church of God to him, than he began his attacks upon it in good earnest. Even while Chancellor, S. Thomas had earnestly entreated the king to fill up the vacant bishoprics with canonically-appointed pastors, and thereby put an end to the abuse which had been so common under the Norman monarchs of keeping their revenues in the royal treasury. Perhaps King Henry was willing to show some special favour to his old friend on his first taking the command of the Church in England; for we read that two fitting bishops were appointed to the sees of Worcester and

Gloucester. But the annoyance Henry showed at the resignation of the chancellorship by the archbishop, would surely go far to show us what the king had expected of him whom he had thus elevated to the Primacy, and how much he hoped that he had a State bishop who would further, and not oppose, his attempts against the liberties of the Church.

Under pretence of the better government of his kingdom, and prevention of many disorders, King Henry required that the clergy who broke the laws, or were guilty of any crime, should be degraded from their orders by the archbishop or bishops, and delivered over to the king's courts of justice for corporal punishment from the civil magistrate: the king also contended that he was the fitting person to give away Church benefices, and to keep their revenues while they were vacant; and it followed, of course, that if the king were in want of money he would not hurry himself to fill up such vacancies. No one in holy orders was to leave the country without the king's leave. No one holding an appointment from the Crown or any of the royal household, were to be subject to the Church's chastisements without the king's leave. Appeals amongst the clergy were to go through the different degrees from archdeacon to bishop, and thence to archbishop, whence they could not go further without the king's leave, who thus effectually stopped appeals to the Pope and reference to Rome, the mother of all the Churches of Christendom. This was the purport and outline of the celebrated Constitutions of Clarendon, so far as they affected the Church; nor was it probable that a man clear sighted as S. Thomas, with the views of a growing Saint as to the rights of the Spouse of Christ, would consent to see her thus in bonds under his archiepiscopate. The bishops were summoned and commanded by the king to promise that they would in all things observe and conform to the "royal customs," the ancient laws and customs of his kingdom, of which these Constitutions of Clarendon were alleged to be part, and which he urged had been sanctioned by long usage under his predecessors. Nor was Henry without support even amongst the clergy; and this brings us to the subject of one of the bishops, whose part was so prominent in the contest which ensued, that a few words must be said upon his character.

Gilbert Foliot, Bishop of London, was originally a monk of the order of Clugni, who after becoming prior of his monastery, was made successively abbot of the Benedictine abbey of S. Peter, Gloucester, Bishop of Hereford, and finally advanced to the see of London. He was a man of considerable austerity of life and reputation for sanctity; indeed on the former point the Pope himself had remonstrated with him, as carrying his self-severity too far for his health, and even endangering his life; but he had one most suspicious element in his character, which was a sort of key-note by which we may almost be sure as to the part he would take in such a contest as the present, and which generally shows unmistakably the difference between the true Shepherd and hireling. Gilbert Foliot, though living the life of an ascetic, yet dreaded above all things the loss of the royal favour. No doubt he did not definitely put before his mind that this was a worse evil than the loss of the favour of the King of Heaven; but just as S. Thomas dreaded the bare chance of offending God in pleasing the king, so the Bishop of London grew distressed and found his conscience driven into a corner when the two duties appeared to clash. An instance of this occurred in a dispute between a dependant of one of the nobility and a small community of monks near London, who had been deprived of their farm by this man, which being referred to the Pope, he had ordered the Bishop to obtain immediate restitution or to excommunicate the offending party and his patron. The offender would not give up the farm, and to excommunicate the noble without the king's licence, which Henry would not give, would entail terrible consequences.

The Bishop seems driven to distraction by the alternative. "Rather," he says, "would I have been without my bishopric than incur either of these calamities; either of the swords which hang over me is heavy, one of which kills the soul, the other the body; the former indeed heavier, *but the latter is by no means light.* . . . If, indeed the cause were one in which death or exile could be worthily undergone, gladly would I face either in compliance with my lord the Pope's wishes. But surely six miserable monks dwelling together in Pauteney, without any rule or order, are not of such importance, that to obtain for them a few acres of land, the Chief Priest of Christendom should interrupt his friendly relations with the king of England."* This melancholy exhibition of the poor Bishop's views prepares us for his conduct in the battle before

* Froude, p. 44.

us, and shows us how truly it is the heart of a man which is everything before the eyes of the all-seeing God; it was this heart which was so true in S. Thomas of Canterbury, even amidst his earlier shortcomings, and so false in Gilbert of London, though surrounded with fasts and prayers.

Certain it is that with that curious instinct with which "those who are of this world" find each other out, and cleave together, Henry singled out this bishop as one of his chief aids in the coming struggle, while he as intuitively stood by the king.

The Council of Westminster was the first holden by the king to propose and enforce his claims on the Church; and here S. Thomas first realized the weakness of his suffragans, none of whom were prepared to stand by him in the coming struggle. S. Thomas put before them that the liberty of the Church was in peril. "Let the liberty of the Church perish, lest we perish ourselves," was their reply; "much must be yielded to the malice of the times." This was an allusion to the German antipope. The reply roused S. Thomas's zeal. "Who hath bewitched you, O foolish bishops! Much must be yielded to the malice of the time, I grant; but are we to add sin to sin? It is when the Church is in trouble, and not merely in times of peace, that a bishop must dare to do his duty. It was not more meritorious for bishops of old to give their blood for the Church than it is now to die in defence of her liberty. I declare, God be my witness, that it is not safe for us to leave that form which we have received from our holy fathers."

Thus the archbishop made known to his brethren of the Episcopate, the high and saintly principles which should animate those whom God has called to be the guardians of His Church and Her rights. But the whole flock of bishops quailed with fear, and "straightway," says one of his old historians, "you might see all the pillars of the Church to tremble as reeds before the wind" (of the king's wrath). Nor did anything support them against the terrors with which they were threatened except the firmness of his Lordship of Canterbury.

The king did not fail to bring what personal remonstrance could effect on his former favourite to bend him to his wishes, and Roger of Pontigni gives an account of this in an interview King Henry had with the Saint after the Council of Westminster, when the former reminded him of his having raised him from a mean station to the highest dignities of his kingdom, and reproached him with forgetting his affection, and showing ingratitude in thus turning against him, to which the Saint made this beautiful reply: '" Far be it from me, my lord; I am not ungrateful for the favours which I received, not from yourself alone, but from God, through you; wherefore far be it from me to resist your will as long as it agrees with the will of God. Your worthiness knows how faithful I have been to you from whom I look but for an earthly reward; how much more then must I do faithful service to Almighty God, from whom I have received what is temporal, and hope for what is eternal! You are my lord, but He is your Lord and mine, and it would be good for neither of us that I should leave His will for yours; for in the awful judgment we shall both be judged as the servants of our Lord, and one will not be able to answer for the other. We must obey our temporal lords, but not against God, for S. Peter says we must obey God rather than man."

To this the king replied that he did not want him to preach him a sermon just then, and asked him if he was not the son of one of his rustics. S. Thomas answered, "In truth I am not sprung of royal race; no more was blessed Peter, the Prince of the Apostles, on whom the Lord deigned to confer the keys of heaven and the headship of the universal Church." "True," said the king, "but he died for his Lord." The primate replied, "I too will die for my Lord when the time comes."

The soul of Henry Plantagenet was cankered to its very core by worldly ambition and the greatness of this world, and it is worth while here to contemplate his character as contrasted with that of Thomas à

Becket. For it is well known that Henry the Second has always born the character of a great king, and of a great man, according to the standard of this world's greatness. Yet such was the fashion of his greatness that he could not even comprehend the true and only real grandeur and dignity which belongs to the children of light. To such a mind an increase of that which he held to be the one great object of existence, worldly power and dominion, was the only motive to which he could attribute so great a change as the feelings and views of the former chancellor had undergone: and while he measured his friend by the same earthly standard, asking him if he had not raised him from the ranks of the vassals to the highest dignity of the realm, as it were to bring to his senses one who seemed to him to be aiming at something above his sovereign, he no doubt regarded him, as do so often souls unable to see through the mist of worldliness into the minds of the true children of the Catholic Church, as sacrificing to ambition a friendship, and stifling an affection which the deep piety and high devotion now embraced by S. Thomas would but have purified and exalted. That much of S. Thomas's great regard for Henry remained even through the cruel and bitter persecution he underwent from that prince, we have most touching instances of, and amongst others one of a vision S. Thomas had concerning him, and which he related during his exile to Herbert de Boscham, to whom, he added, that he should yet help Henry in some of his troubles. Of such a character is the affection of saints. While the king treated with the bitterest resentment and cruelty everything belonging to the man whose regard he held to have cooled towards him. Of such a character is the affection of men of the world.*

* The vision was thus related by S. Thomas to his faithful follower, Herbert de Boscham. "I thought I stood," said the Saint, "on a very high mountain, and the king was in the plain beneath; when on a sudden I saw flying towards him all manner of birds of prey, which with their beaks and talons attacked him violently, and tore his royal robes off him, leaving him half stripped. There was a dark precipice behind him which he did not see, and towards which he was approaching as he was driven backwards by the onset of the birds of prey. When he was in this strait, one of the courtiers, whom the king had trusted and advanced to high places, turned his hand against him, tried to tear from him the rags the birds had spared, and to urge him over the precipice. The thought then came over me of all our old friendship; and coming down from my high mountain-top, as it seemed to me in the twinkling of an eye, his peril and my compassion giving me wings, I was by his side. I had, I know not how, a lance in my hand, and I scattered the birds of prey, and clad the king in his royal robes once more, chiding the while the courtier who had shown such ingratitude, saying that of him at least the king had not merited such treatment." The

The Council of Clarendon was then summoned by the king in order to enforce if possible a public acceptance of "his customs," the Council of Westminster having shown a public opposition to them. And in order to terrify the bishops into submission he filled the council chamber with armed men.

Meanwhile several of the bishops and some of the most powerful lay noblemen, seeing matters coming to great extremities, went to S. Thomas, and urged him for the sake of peace to pacify the king by promis-

king when hearing from Herbert the relation of this vision pressed to know the name of the courtier, but the latter being still alive Herbert refused to tell him. On several occasions King Henry recognised and acknowledged with tears, amidst the terrible troubles of the dark latter years of his life, the powerful aid and intercession of that friend whom he had persecuted unto death.

ing to observe the customs; assuring him that it was merely a question of words, and the king's personal dignity, which he did not like should appear worsted in the contest, and that he would never think of enforcing his demands.

Influenced by their protestations and entreaties, almost against his better judgment, S. Thomas went to the king, and with that beautiful simplicity and confiding ingenuousness which formed part of his character, and made him ready to hope that the king would deal with him as he would with the king, he told him, that trusting in his sovereign's prudence and moderation, he would promise in good faith to observe the customs.

Whatever may be thought of this action of the Saint's, which some have stigmatized as weakness and imprudence, and not perhaps wholly without grounds, the very fault proves at least that he was not opposing the king in a spirit of obstinacy, or contumaciously standing out for the last iota of his claims, but rather that he stretched every point which he thought could consist with the honour of God to keep peace with his royal master—nay, on this occasion he went beyond his conscience in the effort.

The king having gained thus much from his primate, required the other bishops to follow his example, ordered the constitutions to be reduced to writing, and gave evidence that he was going to enforce them in good earnest to their fullest extent. They were read aloud, and the Archbishop for the first time mastered the extent of their evil influence. S. Thomas saw his mistake, and on the king's demanding that he and the bishops should affix their seals to the constitution, he answered at once " By the Lord

Almighty, during my lifetime seal of mine shall never touch them."

As S. Thomas rode away from the court, however, wrapped in deep meditation, apart from his suite, his attendants began to talk over the events of the day, and his cross-bearer, Alexander Llewellen, expressed himself strongly to the effect that the tempest had overthrown the columns of the Church, and that during the shepherd's folly the sheep were scattered before the wolf.

"To whom does this apply, my son?" said the Archbishop. "It applies to you," replied Llewellen, "who have to-day betrayed your conscience and your fame, and in an example hateful to God, and contrary to justice, have stretched out your consecrated hands to observe impious constitutions, and have joined with wicked ministers of Satan to the overthrow of the liberty of the Church."

These words brought before the Saint his own conduct in the same feelings of keen and bitter repentance as are described in the Prince of the Apostles when he denied his Master; and scarce was he consoled by his faithful Herbert, who did all that lay in his power to assuage his grief, by reminding him of the great Scriptural penitents who rose again to yet greater faith after their fall than before. He declared himself unworthy of the sacred office he filled, interdicted himself from saying Mass for 40 days, and, writing to the Pope in deepest sorrow and shame for his fault, he begged for absolution at his hands. But the king, now finding that S. Thomas had resumed his resolution, took another course to grind his opponent to the earth.

During the period of his chancellorship much, or rather the whole, of the royal treasury had been under his control. As the king's prime minister, he had regulated the payment of his troops and other expenses after wars in which Henry had been engaged, and the repairs of the fortresses and places of defence injured during the civil struggles in the reign of Stephen, and though he had lawfully accounted for all the money thus spent to the king before relinquishing his chancellorship, Henry set to work to discover some plea by which he could allege that these moneys had not been lawfully spent, and thus inflict temporal ruin on the man whom as long as he had been his instrument, he thought he could never load with riches enough. He began by accusing S. Thomas of showing contempt of his summons when cited to answer to the charges brought against him on a certain day when the archbishop was too ill to appear. In vain the true cause was stated to the king and parliament; the latter, willing no doubt to conciliate their master, sentenced the archbishop to the confiscation of all his movable goods, or in other words, to a fine of £500. To this the noble and generous mind of S. Thomas, feeling that self alone would suffer the loss, at once declared that a mere question of money should never be a cause of discord between himself and his sovereign, and bail was found for payment of the sum. But the king was not going to let go his prey thus easily, and he next put forward in succession demands not only for large sums spent as chancellor in the ways we have alluded to, but also made heavy demands on Church property and lands, and S. Thomas, feeling that it was the

Spouse of Christ that was now attacked in his person, thought proper to resist. It was at the Council of Northampton that these claims were urged most fully, and for the last time. For this council S. Thomas prepared with extreme solemnity. He entered the church and said the mass of S. Stephen at the Altar of the Protomartyr with very great solemnity and devotion, his tears blinding him so much that he was obliged frequently to break off the prayers unfinished. Two things were particularly noted in this Mass by the king's party: that he had chosen one the Introit of which began with the words, " For the princes sat and spoke against me;" and that he celebrated, though it was not a festival, with his pallium, which was unusual. It also shows the conviction he had of the solemnity and awfulness of the trial he was about to go through, that he carried the Blessed Sacrament concealed on his person into the council-chamber. The Saint would have gone to the Court vested as he came out from Mass, but that he was persuaded by some of his friends not to do so. His wish was, he said, to let the Court see who he was whom it (a lay tribunal) had twice judged. He was persuaded to lay aside his mitre and pallium; and he threw his black cappa over the sacred vestments. But this concession, small as it was, to worldly wisdom he seems to have thought too much, for on his way to the castle he said to his cross-bearer, Llewellen, that he regretted he had not come as he at first proposed. On entering the castle it was observed that he carried his own cross, and on some one saying to the Bishop of London, whom they met in the gateway, "My Lord of London, why do you suffer him to carry his cross?" Gilbert Foliot answered, "Good man, he always was a fool and always will be." And no doubt Gilbert was right, speaking from his own point of view; for the children of this world are wiser in their generation than the children of light, who become fools for the kingdom of Heaven's sake.

The Bishop of Hereford then offered his services as cross-bearer, but the Archbishop declined them, and holding his cross, most truly indeed his strength and his salvation against the powers of this world and of darkness, he entered the council-chamber. Foliot of London, apparently with instinctive uneasiness at this public manifestation of the power and authority of the Church over that of the world, said to him, "You carry your cross; now if the king were to draw his sword, what hope would there be of peace?" S. Thomas replied, "If it could be so, I should wish always to carry it in my own hands; but I know what I am now doing. I would preserve God's peace for myself and the Church in England. Say, if you like, that if you were here you would think otherwise. If my lord the king were now, as you say, to draw his sword, it would be but a bad token of peace." S. Thomas would recognize no peace that was purchased at the price of bondage for the Church of God, yet he aimed at the highest peace— Glory to God, and peace to men of good will. The Bishop of London would fain have cried peace where there was none.

The king, who on the Saint's entrance, had passed into an inner room with his barons, and had been followed by the bishops, at once took up the matter of the cross as an affront, and declared that thus carrying it (the sign of their common salvation, be it observed) was to treat him as if he were not a Christian king. The courtiers of course followed the key-note of their master, and giving the archbishop the appellation of traitor, the murmurs and threats became so loud as to be heard in the adjacent chamber, and the most imminent personal danger to the Saint and his friends seemed impending, so much so, that he and those around him made the sign of the cross.

His faithful chaplain, Herbert de Boscham, with his characteristic ardour and impetuosity, urged him to have his sentence of excommunication ready if his person should be attacked; but Ralph Fitzstephen entreated him rather to imitate the Apostles and Martyrs, and die praying for his murderers, and when forbidden by the king's marshal to speak to the Saint, Fitzstephen made signs to him to look up at the crucifix, and occupy himself in prayer. For this piety and charity years afterwards, when S. Thomas was an exile in France, he gratefully thanked his friend, telling him how he had understood his signs, and what consolation they had brought him. And now as the threats of the courtiers and king's officers grew fiercer in the council-room, S. Thomas, stooping down, expressed his fears for his chaplain, Herbert, yet told him to take heart, for that he should share in his crown of martyrdom. The intrepid Herbert replied, "We must neither of us fear, for you have raised a noble standard by which the powers not only of the earth, but of the air, are overthrown; and remember," added he, "that you were once the standard-bearer of the King of the Angles, and were never overcome : it would indeed be a disgrace to be overcome now, when you are the standard-bearer of the 'King of the Angels.'" These anecdotes will serve to show us the piety and exalted principle of at least some of the priests of an age which has been spoken of by Protestant historians as one of universal corruption and laxity amongst the clergy.

While the king and his nobles were thus preparing to accuse and pass sentence upon the archbishop, the bishops were holding anxious counsel, agitated with the conflicting feelings of fear of the king's wrath on the one side, and disobedience and audacity towards their primate on the other, should they be compelled to join in the sentence. In order as they hoped to avoid both evils, they begged the king to allow them to absent themselves during the judgment on their archbishop, offering to appease the king by appealing to Rome against him, and not to rest until he was deposed; and they told Henry how the archbishop had appealed to Rome against their former sentences. Henry then sent some of his barons into the adjacent chamber to S. Thomas to ask whether, being his (the king's) liege subject, he dared thus appeal, and if he would give bail for the payment of the moneys claimed from him by the king, and abide by the sentence of the Court regarding the expenditure during his chancellorship. S. Thomas replied in a dignified address, in which he explained to the king that he obeyed him for God's sake in all things saving obedience to God, the Church's dignity, and the honour of a bishop; and with graceful acknowledgments of the many honours, dignities, and offices conferred upon

him by his monarch, in all of which he had
served him faithfully on both sides of the
Channel, he rejoiced to think that after
spending all his income in the royal service,
he had incurred debts for the king also. He
declined to be held answerable for the trans-
actions of his chancellorship, since he was,
he said, as both the king and clergy well
knew—though the former now in his anger
refused to admit it,—declared by the king at
his election free from all secular obligations:*

* When Henry made his last iniquitous demand on
S. Thomas, that he should account for the incomes of
all the vacant bishoprics and abbacies which had been
paid into the Chancery while he was in office, Henry of
Blois, the generous old Bishop of Winchester, reminded
the king of the manner in which he had freed the Archbishop at his election from all secular claims, through
the prince who declared it in his father's name in his,
the bishop's presence. Finding, however, that the king
obstinately refused to recognize any liberation, he offered
the latter two thousand marks on S. Thomas's behalf;

that he had indeed appealed against the bishops, whom he had forbidden as his spiritual children to judge him for a secular cause which occurred before he was archbishop; and he placed his person and the Church of Canterbury under the protection of God and the Pope.

When the king got this reply, which was received by the fierce barons with threats audible to the archbishop in the adjoining chamber, Henry urged the bishops to join in the sentence to be pronounced against S. Thomas: but after some debate he allowed them to absent themselves, and they all rejoined the archbishop in the antechamber except the Archbishop of York, who, not wishing as he said to witness the slaughter of the Primate, or perhaps

but Henry, whose real object was to ruin his former favourite, refused them.

frightened for his own safety, managed to withdraw altogether.

The Bishop of Chichester then addressed S. Thomas, urging him to yield, and reproaching him for going back from what he had promised at Clarendon in good faith. To which S. Thomas answered, that whatever was against the Church or the laws of God could not be kept in good faith: "Furthermore," said he, "if we fell at Clarendon, for the flesh is weak, we must take courage, and in the strength of the Holy Ghost contend against the ancient enemy who is ever striving to make him fall who stands, and to prevent him from rising who has fallen. If then in the word of truth we swore to what was unjust, you know that an unlawful oath is not binding."

The Bishop of Exeter threw himself at the Saint's feet and implored him to have pity on himself and the bishops, for the king had, he said, just decreed that any one taking S. Thomas's part should be judged guilty of high treason. "Fly hence," said the Saint to the suppliant Prelate, "for you savour not the things that be of God." After some further discussion,—in which the Bishops tried in vain to wring from the Primate permission to obey the king in being present at the sentence about to be pronounced against him,—the barons entered the apartment, headed by Robert Earl of Leicester and Reginald Earl of Cornwall, and the former desired the archbishop to hear his judgment. "Judgment!" said the archbishop, rising up, "Son and Earl, hear me first. You know, my son, how intimate I was with our lord the king, and how faithfully I served him. It therefore pleased him that I should be advanced to be Archbishop of the Church of Canterbury. God knows I willed it not, for I knew my own weakness, and rather for the love of him than of God I gave way, which to-day is clear enough, when God and the king have both deserted me. Still in my promotion, when I was elected before Henry, the king's son and heir, the question was asked, How did they give me to the Church of Canterbury? And the answer was, Free from all worldly ties. Therefore I am not bound, nor will I plead respecting them." The Earl of Leicester then declared that the Bishop of London had given a different account of this matter to the king; but urged that as the archbishop held many castles and possessions of that monarch in fief and barony, he did not see how he could avoid the king's judgment. The archbishop replied that he held nothing in fief or barony, for that whatever kings gave to the Church was given as a free alms, and that the king in his privileges had confirmed the same; and he forbade the Earl of Leicester, by his sacred authority, to pass judgment upon him. The Earl upon this, unwilling, no doubt, to risk his salvation to such an extent and to incur excommunication, declined proceeding further, as did the Earl of Cornwall, but they entreated the archbishop to wait until the king's answer was brought to him. The archbishop asked if he was a prisoner, and the Earl of Leicester swearing by S. Lazarus that he was not, S. Thomas added, "Son and Earl, yet listen. By as much as the soul is more worthy than the body, by so much are you bound to obey God and me, rather than your earthly king. Neither law nor reason permits children to judge and condemn their father. Wherefore I decline the king's judgment and yours; and under God will be judged by the Pope alone, to whom before you all I here appeal, placing the Church of Canterbury, my order, and my dignity under God and His protection. And you, my brethren and fellow bishops, who have served man rather than God, I summon to the presence of the Pope, and so guarded by the authority of the Catholic Church and of the Holy See I go hence." And so, with all the grandeur of Apostolic dignity about him, the Saint, still bearing his cross, left the council-chamber. There were not wanting persons to insult him as he passed out; the de Brocs, noblemen of the worst character and reputation, and others of the king's followers, threw knots of straw and other such things after him, and one of them calling him traitor, roused the old martial spirit of S. Thomas, who turned a stern countenance upon his accuser, and said if his priesthood did not prevent him, he would defend himself in arms from their charges of perjury and treason.

In the court of the castle he mounted his horse and rode back to the Monastery of S. Andrew, amidst the benedictions of the populace and many of the clergy, who seem to have been waiting in terror for the fate of their friend and benefactor. All as he approached raised a loud cry: "Blessed be God, who has saved his servant from the face of his enemies." So great was the throng that the Saint could hardly guide his horse and hold his cross, as he blessed the crowds who fell upon their knees as he passed. Truly it was, as he called it, a glorious procession, for, like his Divine Master, the poor were ever his special friends and care, and they dined with him that day in great numbers.

Thus ended the celebrated Council of Northampton, which took place on a Tuesday, that day of the week which always marked the chief events of S. Thomas's life.

Lingard says that it was generally believed that if the archbishop had remained in Northampton, that night would have proved the last of his life on earth. Many well-authenticated reports as to the king's intended vengeance upon one whom he chose to account a rebel had reached S. Thomas, who took as a sort of heavenly warning a sentence which occurred in the spiritual reading during supper. It was the history of the persecution of Liberius from the tripartite ecclesiastical history, and the words were "When they persecute you in one city fly to another." The Saint and Herbert interchanged looks, and his flight was tacitly agreed upon between them. This resolution seems to have been confirmed by the circumstance of S. Thomas's sending that evening the Bishops of Worcester, Hereford, and Rochester to the king, to ask for leave for S. Thomas to depart on the morrow, and a safe conduct for him to visit the Pope, when the king refused to give any answer until the next day.

Out of the forty followers who had passed into the council-chamber with the Saint, but six remained to sit down with him to this, as it may truly be called, "Feast of the poor"; so powerful are the wishes of the rulers of this world over the hearts of the children of earth; nor must we omit the words of exhortation addressed by S. Thomas to these few faithful friends, breathing as they do the saintly spirit of the speaker at every word. "Dwell in silence and in peace," he said to them. "Let no sharp word proceed from your mouth. If any one speak against you, do not answer him, but suffer him to speak evil of you. The superior part is to suffer, the inferior so to act. We are masters of our own ears as they are of their tongues. The evil is not spoken against me; but against him who when evil is spoken recognizes it in himself."

Late at night, in darkness and a heavy rain falling, S. Thomas escaped on horseback from Northampton; the gates of which town had all been guarded by the king (no doubt to secure his captive) save one which one must think had been overlooked by a special interposition of Divine Providence Who willed that His servant's hour was not yet come. After various vicissitudes, adventures, and hair-breadth escapes, he reached Sandwich, crossed the sea in a small boat on All Souls' Day, Nov. 2nd, and landed on a part of the French coast near Gravelines, whence he proceeded, not without renewed dangers and hardships, to the Monastery of S. Bertin, where Herbert and other friends joined him. His escape in safety, first through the dominions of his powerful foe Henry who had sent watchers and pursuers to all parts, and secondly through those of the Earl of Boulogne who hated him for having while chancellor opposed a sacrilegious marriage the earl made with the Abbess of Romsey, can hardly be regarded as less than miraculous. One of the archbishop's followers whom he had left behind at Northampton told Herbert that he had that night a dream in which he heard a voice sing the words from the Psalm, " Our soul has escaped like a sparrow from the snare of the fowlers: our snare is broken and we are delivered."

Our present article is purely biographical and not doctrinal or historical. We will not therefore attempt, as might so easily be done, to show the vital importance towards the Church's highest interests whether of the ecclesiastical immunities,* or of the other great principles for which S. Thomas contended. In the present age, when the course of thought is beginning to free itself

* The 30th error condemned in the Syllabus is that "the immunity of the Church and of ecclesiastical persons had its origin from the civil law." The 31st that "the ecclesiastical forum for the temporal causes of clerics should be altogether abolished, even without consulting, and against the protest of, the Apostolic See." An admirable exposition of the Church's whole doctrine on the subject will be found in the fourth book of Suarez's " Defensio Fidei Catholicæ."

from the iron cramps and fetters of the so-called Reformation, even sceptics regard the Church of the middle ages with very different eyes from the Protestant historians of the last century, and we find them speaking thus of a subject which has so excited the sectarian wrath of a Hume or a Goldsmith : " Even for what seems in the abstract a still more objectionable pretension, the claim to the exemption of ecclesiastics from secular jurisdiction, which has scandalized so grievously most of our English historians, there is much more to be said than those historians were aware of. What was it, after all, but the assertion in behalf of the clergy, of the received English principle of being tried by their peers ? The secular tribunals were the courts of a rival power often in actual conflict with the clergy, always jealous of them, always ready to make use of its jurisdiction as a means of wreaking its vengeance or serving its ambition; and were stained besides with the grossest corruption and tyranny." The same writer, Mr. Stuart Mill, speaks of the Catholic Church of the middle ages as being "the authorized champion of intelligence and self-control against military and predatory violence," and "the great improver and civilizer of Europe." Certainly no one can read the letters of S. Thomas of Canterbury and the ecclesiastics of his time, without being struck with them as the compositions of men of the highest education; while our boasted Henry Plantagenet, though no doubt better informed than most of his barons, comes out as a rough barbarian. The judicial courts of the State being therefore of the corrupt character we have described in that age, were peculiarly unfit to sit in judgment upon Churchmen. Too much had already been conceded in England by S. Thomas's predecessors; some of whom had sought to mitigate the evil of the perpetual encroachments of the State on the Church's rights by a spirit of compromise: and it was clear to S. Thomas, on the perusal of the Constitutions of Clarendon, that if enforced they would have brought bonds and subjection to the Church. He saw that it depended on the issue of this contest as to whether the Catholic Church should continue as before to teach her children Christianity, to model their minds in the paths of piety and the highest improvement and civilization,—or become the slave of the State letting in the floods of anarchy, confusion, and schism which then especially attended temporal powers. Measures therefore so subversive of the Kingdom of

Christ upon earth must be resisted unto blood.

And now that we have followed S. Thomas to this great epoch in his history we may pause to contemplate the working of God's grace on the great soul it pleased Him to call to so lofty a destiny; for it is from this period that the real history of S. Thomas of Canterbury begins. In reading the life of this great servant of God, which is so varied in its scenes and incidents as to resemble a romance, and so mixed up with the politics both religious and secular of the age as to form a part of the history of England, we might say of Europe, we are naturally drawn to contemplate with earnest gaze the external events surrounding him who stands out as the hero of a most eventful period. And there is so much to arrest our attention and enlist our sympathy in his changeful fortunes, —so much to justify the titles of saint and martyr in his external troubles and the cause in support of which he met his death,—that we are apt to lose sight of his interior life in a greater measure than is the case in reading the life of a saint whose earthly existence was passed in scenes of a more tranquil and everyday character. Yet this is in truth the only true history of S. Thomas of Canterbury; and it will be our wish in these pages to dwell rather on the effect produced on the mind of the Saint by the events by which he was surrounded and the trials sent by God for his greater purification, than on those events and trials themselves, described as they have already been by so many more learned and able writers than the present.

To watch the gold of the souls of the saints as stage after stage it is first softened by the heat of trial and grief, then melted by the fierce flames of bitterness and persecution,—different degrees in the fire of His great crucible Who refines the souls of His elect until they are moulded by their last deep and great suffering into the image of the Crucified, —is truly to read and contemplate the lives of saints, and it is thus that we desire to deal with that of S. Thomas.

The great highway of the cross was now full before our Saint. Stripped of all his earthly possessions, disgraced and degraded, so far as he could do it, by the very man to whose service he had given the best years of his life and strength, he was driven forth to wander an exile in a foreign land. This was in itself hardship enough : for S. Thomas was not a Norman noble, but a complete Englishman, in his feelings at least ; and the constant yearnings he had after his native country, notwithstanding the kind hospitality of the French, formed one of the bitterest drops in the chalice of suffering which awaited him.

King Henry heard of his victim's escape with anger too deep for utterance. When he could express himself he said, "We have not yet done with him." He then selected a body of bishops and nobles to repair to the Pope to make the appeal promised on the part of the former against S. Thomas. Of course all the Saint's bitterest opponents were selected, and amongst them Gilbert of London. The King also wrote letters to the King of France and the Earl of Flanders, begging them not to receive into their dominions a traitor whom he called the *late* Archbishop of Canterbury.

Both the archbishop's party and the king's were bound to Sens, where the Pope then was; and S. Thomas having found fresh danger from Henry's machinations with the Earl of Flanders, in the territories of that Prince, had proceeded to Soissons, where he was in the dominions of the King of France. There he remained while Herbert and another of his suite were sent on to the Pope, waiting on the King of France on their road. Pope Alexander had taken up his abode in the city of Sens in consequence of the struggle which was going on between him and the antipope, a contest of which Henry did not fail to make good use in his battle with S. Thomas.

Such was the history of persecution, trial, and suffering which Herbert and his companion on their arrival at Sens had to relate to the Holy Father of their archbishop, that the Pope said, weeping, "Your lord is yet alive, you tell me; he can then while still in the flesh claim the privilege of martyrdom."

If we wanted proof of the heroic tenderness of our Saint, that "liquefaction of the heart," as some one expresses it in speaking of the Curé d'Ars, possessed by the saints, we should find it in S. Thomas's deep feeling and affection for his friends and those who walked with him in the steep and rugged road of the cross ; for whom throughout his wanderings and exile he was always feeling more than for himself, and whose privations and sufferings on his account went near to break a spirit which seemed to rise indomitable above its own sharpest afflictions. And the attachment to him of Herbert his chaplain, John of Salisbury his friend, and the Prior of Merton his former tutor, and indeed of all those with whom he had been associated in the more intimate relations of life, was unbounded and enthusiastic.

The bishops and king's messengers made

their appearance at Sens about the same time as the friends of the archbishop; and both on this and every succeeding occasion in the negotiations between the contending parties, the bishops spared no pains to misrepresent the conduct of the archbishop to the Roman authorities. He was, they said, hasty, overbearing, intolerant, and obstinate; or, as the Bishop of London expressed it on a later occasion, "he strikes before he threatens, suspends and excommunicates before he admonishes." While on the other hand they spoke of our fierce and absolute Plantagenet, as if he were a meek, gentle, much-injured monarch, only seeking his own rights and the good government of his kingdom. But Gilbert Foliot could not keep charity in speaking of his rival, so that on one occasion the Pope called out to him to "spare." The bishop misunderstanding him said, "Shall I spare him, my Lord?" "Brother," said the Holy Father, "I said not spare *him*, but *thyself;*" on which Foliot held his tongue with confusion.

The Pope, however, was aware of the real characters of the persons with whom he had to deal in this great controversy; as is clearly shown in a letter written by him to this very Gilbert Foliot, about the end of 1165 or early in 1166.

Hereby, then, we warn and charge you to choose an early opportunity, such as your intimacy with his Majesty the King of England will doubtless afford you, of laying before his Majesty the heinous nature of his conduct. You are to bid him discontinue the practice in which he has hitherto persisted, of confusing secular and ecclesiastical causes, so that the affairs of the Church may henceforth be arranged by churchmen, and none but matters strictly civil be brought before his Majesty's judges. Moreover, he is forthwith to receive our venerable brother the Archbishop of Canterbury with the honour due to his station, and to reinstate him, together with his fellow exiles, in their former rights and possessions. .... Moreover, you yourself are to render to the See of Canterbury that submission which is due from you to Christ, inasmuch as the things of Cæsar are due to Cæsar, and the things of God to God.*

In another letter to the same person the Pope seems still more fully to see that his Lordship of London, as well as his patron, were to be distrusted.

THE POPE TO THE BISHOP OF LONDON.

Statements are frequently made to us respecting you, which consist ill with your monastic character and exterior deportment, and which, if substantiated, must shake our confidence in the sincerity of your professions.

It is not gratitude, nor love, nor fear, that will justify you in the neglect of your sacred functions, and in abandoning the cause of the Church. Rather ought you to stand forth with manly constancy as its firmest pillar, fearing God and not man. Remember that when wicked men oppress the Church, the truest love would lead you not merely to protest against them, but to raise your voice unceasingly, as it were a trumpet; always remembering the prophet's words. "Nisi annunciaveritis iniquo iniquitatem suam, sanguinem ejus de manu tuâ requiram."

* Froude, p. 110.

Meantime the King of England wrote thus to his friend, on hearing of the well-earned spiritual censures with which the primate had visited his rebellious suffragan :—

THE KING TO THE BISHOP OF LONDON.

I have heard of the grievance which that traitor Thomas, my adversary, has inflicted on you and other dignitaries of my realm ; nor am I less indignant at this outrage in your case than if he had vomited out his poison against myself. Be assured that I shall use all my influence with his Lordship the Pope, and the King of France, and all my friends among the Cardinals, that he may be disabled from doing ourself and our realm any further injury.*

The Bishop of London was especially pleasing to Henry from his envy of S. Thomas, which had led him from the first to put forward certain claims which he contended the See of London had over the Archbishopric of Canterbury : London having

* Froude.

been, he said, in early times, before the introduction of Christianity, the chief city of religious worship. Could he have prevailed on Rome to recognize it as the seat of the Primacy, and himself in consequence as Primate—and he really seems to have had hopes of this,—the whole quarrel would of course have come to an end, and an Archbishop after the King's own heart would have succeeded to S. Thomas.

John of Salisbury speaks with force, joined with much wit, on this subject, and in a letter to the Chapter of Canterbury he writes thus :—

> It is a boast of his [the Bishop of London] that London was in former times the seat of the Archflamen, when the worship of Jupiter prevailed. Perhaps, as he is so wise and religious a person, he would have no objection to see the worship of Jupiter brought back again; and if he cannot be Archbishop, he may at any rate have the name and title of Arch-flamen. He relies on a prophecy of Merlin, who, under some im-

pulse I know not what, foretold, before the coming of S. Augustine into England, that when the dignity of London should be transferred to Dover, the Christian religion would be destroyed and restored again. However the disciple of Merlin, knowing that his master is no mighty authority, has had recourse, they say, to stronger arguments. He reckons upon the power of the prince, and the weakness of the Church; upon the avarice of the Roman Court; upon your pusillanimity; upon the Archbishop's poverty and his own wealth; which he thinks will make him prevail in his vanity against the wisdom and justice of God.*

Foliot's chief strength against his Primate, however, seems to have lain with the King; for most of the other bishops, though weak and wavering in the hour of trial, and terrified from their duty by the royal threats, would not on the whole depart from their allegiance to the See of Canterbury.

It has ever been the policy of the Court of Rome to deal with all her children as a loving mother, whose anxiety is not less, nay

* Froude, p. 425.

is greater, for the erring members of her family, than for those of whose piety and goodness she is sure. Not only was King Henry her child, but he held in his grasp the souls of such myriads of her other children, that she paused ere she struck a blow which might place him and herself in open variance. Henry took all the advantage of this hesitation which could be taken by a wily and cruel foe, to force S. Thomas forward into a concession of those principles for which he was contending.

S. Thomas's first step in his banishment was to resign his Archbishopric into the hands of the Pope, as fearing that his election had been influenced by the King's wishes; but Alexander at once restored it to him, declaring that his conduct had proved him to be the most fit person for that office. He then retired to the Cistercian Monastery of Pontigni, where, by the kindness and favour of the King of France, he had a safe asylum. And while in this retirement, he had time to reflect on the sad state of his spouse, the Church of Canterbury. Exiled, ruined, and separated from her as he was, it must have added no little to his cruel trial to remember that he left her also in the hands of his bitterest enemies, the de Brocs, who speedily possessed themselves of his castle of Saltwode and other manors belonging to him. The King was resolved that his victim should experience the fullest effects of opposing his will; and with a refinement of cruelty, made use of his knowledge of his former favourite's disposition, to invent an appropriate measure of persecution. Well did King Henry know the loving and tender heart of his former Chancellor, and its deep sympathies for those in distress; and rightly did he measure the heroic and unselfish generosity, to which it would be a far more exquisite torment to see others ruined and homeless on his account, than to endure those miseries himself. Putting the de Brocs at the head of this noble enterprise against the helpless and poor, Henry issued a sentence of banishment against all who were connected with the Primate either by blood or friendship.

Four hundred unhappy exiles were sent forth from their hearths. The sentence went out on Christmas-day, as if this sad band should be headed by the Prince of Exiles. And as the crowd of his friends and relatives, and even all who were supposed to adhere to his opinions, were driven to his place of banishment, homeless, destitute, starving, in the dead of winter, under sickness, weakness, and whatever other circumstances could add to the terrors of such a fate, S. Thomas must have realized to the full that interior martyrdom which likens the soul more fully to its Lord than even a violent death for His sake.

Often, while chancellor, had he longed for quiet and retirement to devote himself to sacred studies; and the duties of Archbishop, even, had not permitted him leisure to fulfil his desires in this respect. But now, in the deep retirement of Pontigni, the Saint gave full vent to his thirst for study and prayer; to which he joined all the austerities to which the love of his vehement spirit urged him, burning as it was now in the purifying fires of suffering. He tried to follow all the rigours observed by the severe Cistercians in their diet; and when he became ill from this, he used the cold stream that flowed past the monastery as an instrument of mortification. But these bodily penances, severe as they were, were but the exterior additions to the great interior work, the shaping of the Image of the Crucified in his soul. What he felt at the consideration of the miserable state of his See of Canterbury, and indeed the whole Church in England, in bonds for his sake and under a cruel oppressor, may be seen by the following extracts from some of his letters to Henry, when, being invested with legatine powers by the Pope, he tried to make some impression on the hard heart of his former friend. The gentle, yet solemn, warning tone of these letters must forcibly strike the reader.

THE ARCHBISHOP OF CANTERBURY TO THE KING OF ENGLAND.

To his most revered Lord Henry, by the grace of God the illustrious King of England, Duke of Normandy and Aquitain, and Count of Angers, Thomas by the same grace the humble minister of the Church of Canterbury, health and a holy life.

I entreat you, O my lord, to bear with me for a while, that by the grace of God I may disburden my conscience to the benefit of your soul. I am troubled on all sides; tribulation and anguish have found me out. Whether I speak or keep silence, evil awaits me every way. If I am silent, woe is me, for how shall I escape His hands who saith: "If thou speakest not to warn the wicked from his way, to save his life, his blood will I require at thy hand!" If I speak out, then, I dread the wrath of my lord. Yet it is safer to face the wrath of man, than to fall into the hands of the living God. Therefore, trusting in His mercy, in Whose hands are the hearts of kings, and Who turneth them severally as He will, now that I have broken silence I will speak on. My lord, the daughter of Sion is held captive in thy kingdom. The Spouse of the great King is oppressed by her enemies, afflicted by those who ought most to honour her, and especially by you. O remember what great things God has done for you; release her, reinstate her in her kingdom, and take away the reproach from your generation.

Trust in my words, my beloved lord; God is a judge slow to anger and long-suffering, but an avenger most terrible. Hearken to me and amend your ways, lest some day the Almighty gird His sword upon His thigh and deliver His Spouse with a mighty hand. If it be that you shall hear my words, and prove yourself from this day forward God's faithful soldier, then He will bless you greatly, and give glory to your sons and to your sons' sons. But if not, then truly I dread (may God avert it!) that the sword shall not depart from thy house till the Most High has made clean vengeance for His people. Remember, my lord, how after God had chosen Solomon, and given him wisdom and prosperity, yet because he turned back from the way of God, and repented not in due time of his iniquities, therefore was his kingdom rent from him and given to his servant. Whereas David, his father, obtained pardon because he humbled himself at once, and sought it from the Lord. May my lord the king do likewise.

The second is written in a yet more intimate and affectionate tone of warning and rebuke.

THE ARCHBISHOP OF CANTERBURY TO THE KING OF ENGLAND.

To his Lord and friend Henry, by the grace of God King of England, &c. Thomas, by the same grace, the humble minister of the Church of Canterbury, his own once after the flesh, and now much more in the spirit, may he repent and amend his ways.

Waiting I have waited for the day when God should

turn your Majesty from crooked ways and evil counsels; silently and anxiously have I waited for the tidings of my son and lord the King of England, who was once seduced by the enemies of the Church; being by the grace of God restored to it in abundant humility, and though I wait in vain, still I weary not, but pray for your Majesty day by day.

Yet now am I straitened above measure, for a spiritual power* has been assigned to me by the same God under Whom you hold temporal dominion, and my office constrains me to address your Majesty in a manner which, as yet, my exile has prevented. It is my duty to exhort your Majesty, nay, to warn and rebuke you, lest if in anything you have done amiss, which indeed you have, my silence may endanger my own soul. Consider then, most mighty prince, that the royal power in each separate realm cannot more justly interfere with the polity of Christ's Universal Church, than the private rights of any town in your Majesty's dominions with your Majesty's prerogative. The most ancient usage has established, that in causes where the priesthood is concerned only priests should pronounce judgment. The great Emperor Constantine declined to interfere in such.

---

* S. Thomas here refers to the office of Legate conferred upon him by the Pope, of which we shall speak presently.

Indeed all history teaches us that it is the custom of Christian princes to submit themselves to the Church, not to rule over it; the authority of the priesthood being so much weightier than that of kings, in proportion as they who are entrusted with it have to render their account concerning kings themselves. The Bishop's sentence has before now sufficed to excommunicate king and emperor too. Pope Innocent excommunicated the Emperor Arcadius; S. Ambrose the great Theodosius; and that, too, for a cause which the other clergy deemed a light one. Yet he earned absolution by a notable penance. King David bowed before the prophet Nathan, and obtained pardon. Be converted, then, my beloved son, my royal master, and follow the man after God's own heart.*

These letters to one who had been to S. Thomas, indeed, as he called him, "his beloved son and royal master," and had become his most bitter opponent, evince the cruel anxieties from which our Saint suffered; and the imploring tone of a betrayed and injured friend, joined with the dignified

* Froude, pp. 139, 140, 141.

rebuke of the servant and priest of God to his spiritual and temporal lord, is very touching.

S. Thomas, however, continued to employ his exile in deep communication with his God, and perfecting his soul and preparing it for that bloody crown which it pleased his Lord to forewarn him was awaiting him.

One day while he was praying before the altar of S. Stephen, after having said Mass, he heard a voice calling him twice by his name, "Thomas! Thomas!" "Who art Thou, Lord?" the Saint asked; and the Lord replied, "I am Jesus Christ, thy Lord and Brother; My Church shall be glorified in thy blood, and thou shalt be glorified in Me." The Abbot of Pontigni, who was waiting for S. Thomas, heard the words; but our Saint bound him to secrecy until the words should be fulfilled. Our Lord also sent him a second vision, in which the very circumstances of his martyrdom were portrayed before him so vividly that he seemed overpowered with sorrow and heaviness after it; yet such was the heavenliness of this spirit, now almost purified to take its flight to the realms of peace, that when he was questioned on the subject, it appeared that his sorrow and care was, like his blessed Master's, for those he must leave behind him on earth, rather than for himself.

"But what has a man who eats and drinks to do with martyrdom?" asked the Abbot of the monastery, smiling, of our Saint, in whom he (who was a stranger just come) saw but a man who looked to him like others, while his soul was hid with Christ in God. S. Thomas replied in deepest humility, "I know that I am too fond of worldly pleasures, but the Lord is good, Who justifies the wicked, and He has deigned to reveal this to me, who am all unworthy."

The persecution of the Saint at the King's hands continued. The monks of Pontigni were now informed that if they continued to harbour King Henry's enemy, that prince would drive all their order out of his dominions. They grieved sorely at having to part with their holy guest, but the royal threats were peremptory, and they had no courage to resist them.

The great enemies and bitterest persecutors of God's Saints become, in fact, their greatest benefactors, as these holy ones are the first to feel; and the meek and gentle patience of S. Thomas, as he discussed with his followers where they could next lay their homeless heads, and his playful remarks to them under this new suffering, remind us of S. Elizabeth's sweet and heroic bearing when she was driven forth homeless by her ruthless brothers-in-law, or was precipitated into the muddy stream by a former object of her charity. And when we remember the passionate temperament, high spirit, and vehement disposition of S. Thomas, we shall see the more clearly the great work which had been effected in his soul by the grace of God. And then came temptations. On one occasion when they met during this long exile, the King said to him, " O why do you not do my will? I certainly would put everything into your hands." Which reminded him, he said, of the passage in Scripture: " All these things will I give thee if thou wilt fall down and worship me."

How many even good people would have thought that here was perhaps an opportunity of reclaiming the King from his evil ways, regaining the old power the Archbishop had over that monarch, and thus by degrees working things round to the ultimate good of the Church. But Saints see things only from one point of view, and that is their Lord's. They regard the events of this life as God regards them, not as man. They keep God's will straight before them, and turn neither to the right hand nor to the left, to follow the sophistries of human prudence. No one realized more fully than our Saint all that he renounced to fight for Christ. "Little should I have needed their patronage," says he, speaking of his enemies, "if I had chosen to forsake the Church and yield to his [the King's] wilfulness myself. I might have flourished in wealth and abundance of delicacies. I might have been feared, courted, honoured, and might have provided for my own in luxury and worldly glory as I pleased. But because God called me to the government of His Church, an unworthy sinner as I was, and most wretched though flourishing in the world's goods beyond my countrymen, through His grace preventing and assisting me, I chose rather to be an outcast from the palace, to be exiled, proscribed, and to finish my life in the last wretchedness, than to sell the Church's liberty, and to prefer the iniquitous traditions of men to the law of God." Then, as it were in a spirit of prophecy, he adds: "For myself, I know that my own days are few; and that unless I declare to the wicked man his ways, his blood will shortly be required at my hands by One from Whom no patronage can protect me. There silver and gold will be profitless, and gifts, that blind the eyes of wise ones. We shall soon stand all of us before the tribunal of Christ, and by His Majesty and terrible judgment I conjure your Holiness, as my Father and Lord, and as the Supreme Judge on earth, to render justice to His Church and to myself, against those who seek my life to take it away."

The King of France, Louis VII., whose name deserves to be gratefully remembered for his early reverence for and appreciation of so great a Saint, came forward on this, as on every other occasion in his power, to the assistance of the Archbishop. On hearing that he was hunted from his retreat at Pontigni by his cruel persecutor, he expressed his surprise and concern at the event, crying out to those near him, " O Religion, O Religion, where art thou? Those whom we believed dead to the world fear its threats, and, professing to despise the things that perish, for their sake turn back from the work of God, which they had taken in hand, and drive God's Exile from them." King Louis then sent him this message by his faithful Herbert:—"Salute your lord the Archbishop," he said, "and promise him in my name that, though the world and those who are dead to the world desert him, I will not. Let him tell us what city or castle, or other place of our dominions, he would prefer, and he shall find it prepared for him." S. Thomas chose the royal Abbey of St. Columba, near Sens, where he remained as the guest of the King of France from St. Martin's day, Nov. 11th, 1166, until his exile was terminated by the crown of martyrdom.

There S. Thomas, still pursuing the penitential life which he had laid down for himself, failed not to continue to do battle for the Church and the rights of the Holy See.

"By a sentence promulgated with more than usual solemnity," says Lingard,* "he cut off from the society of the Faithful such of the royal ministers as had communicated with the antipope, those who had framed the Constitutions of Clarendon, and all who had invaded the property of the Church." When at Vezelay, on his road to Sens from Pontigni, S. Thomas had celebrated High Mass on the festival of Pentecost; and after the Gospel he preached a forcible sermon, in which, with deepest emotion, he warned King Henry by name of the sentence of the Church hanging over him. It is well known that, in the midst of the King's reckless audacity and contumacy, he had still faith enough to dread this sword of the Church above all things. He therefore sent con-

---

* Lingard, vol. ii. p. 230.

stant letters and messengers to Pope Alexander, endeavouring at once to undermine the Primate's character at Rome, and to induce the Pontiff to believe that he was willing to come to an arrangement and be reconciled to S. Thomas; while the Bishop of London, who had himself been punished with excommunication by S. Thomas for his contumacy and disobedience, continued to spare no pains to traduce his Archbishop in the same quarter. It was in the hope of giving a little time to accommodate matters between so powerful a monarch as Henry and the Primate of his dominions, that the Pope had issued the letters of legatine suspension for S. Thomas, of which we are about to speak. For the cup of his sufferings was not yet full, and it remained that they should come upon him in yet greater force than heretofore, from that quarter where his strength lay, and to which his devotion and loyalty were highest.

The course held by Rome and the Holy Father, who now encouraged him, and then, through prudence and caution towards Henry, gave certain advantages to his enemies, tried the Archbishop to the very soul.

Alexander had appointed S. Thomas legate of the Holy See in England, thereby empowering him to exercise spiritual censures against his opponents. The latter, however, no sooner felt his arm lifted against them than they fled to Rome with fresh appeals against him; and finally, backed by the constant and powerful support and threats of King Henry, they obtained the Archbishop's temporary suspension from his office of Legate.

Perhaps, there was no description of

affliction which would have wrung the heart of S. Thomas so keenly as the suspension from his legatine powers by the very hand of that authority to preserve whose rights intact he was suffering exile, want, and all the worst evils of this life. We will hear his account of himself and his sorrows in a letter he wrote on this occasion to the Pope:

> O my Father, my soul is in bitterness; the letters in which your Holiness was pleased to suspend me have made myself and my unhappy fellow-exiles a very scorn of men, and outcast of the people, and what grieves me worse, have delivered up God's Church to the will of its enemies.
> Our persecutor had held out sure hopes to the Earl of Flanders, and others of the French nobility, that he meant to make peace with us. But his messengers arrived with their new powers from your Holiness, and all was at an end. What could our friends do for us when thus repulsed by your Holiness's act, and smitten down as with the club of Hercules? Would that your Holiness's ear could hear what is said of this matter by the bishops, nobles, and commons of both realms; and that your eye could see the scandal with which it has

filled the French court. What is there that this man may not now look for, when, through agents famous only for their crimes, he has circumvented those who have the key of knowledge, overthrown the ministers of justice, and seared the majesty of the Apostolic See? It is no longer doubted that John of Oxford deceived your Holiness, and with impunity; and, surely, to be deceived once in such a matter is inconvenient; nor will the English Church quickly recover from the ill effects of it, dissemble as it may. But that venerable Abbot of St. Augustine's, once a runaway monk for his merits excommunicate, who dilapidates and pollutes the Church he governs, has, with his fellow-envoys, practised a far worse deception. For lo! this King, whose sole hope rests on the chance of your Holiness's death or mine, has obtained the very thing he wishes—a fresh delay, in which one or other of these events may happen; —God avert them.

But your Holiness counsels me to bear with patience the meanwhile. . . .

And do you not observe, O Father, what this "meanwhile" may bring about to the injury of the Church and of your Holiness's reputation? "Meanwhile" the King applies to his own purposes the revenues of the vacant abbeys and bishoprics, and will not suffer pastors to be ordained there. "Meanwhile" he riots in uncontrolled insolence against the parishes, churches, holy places, and the whole sacred order. "Meanwhile," he and the other persecutors of the Church make their will their law. "Meanwhile," who is to take charge of the sheep of Christ, and save them from the jaws of wolves, who no longer prowl around, but have entered the fold and devour and tear, and slay, with none to resist them? For what pastor is there whose voice you have not silenced? What bishop have you not suspended in suspending me?

This act of your Holiness's is alike unexampled and unmerited, and will do the work of tyrants in other days as well as yours. Your Holiness has set an example ready to their hands; and, doubtless, this man and his posterity, unless your Holiness takes steps to ordain otherwise, will draw it into a precedent. He and his nobles, whatever be their crime, will claim, among the privileges of the realm, exemption from any sentence of excommunication or interdict till authorized by the Apostolic See; then, in time, when the evil has taken root, neither will the Chief Priest of Rome himself find any in the whole kingdom to take part with him against the King and his princes.

Another letter to the Pope on the same subject ends thus :—

May your Holiness fare well and be strong; and may

it please you ere long to condescend to my relief, that I, *whose life is a death*, may at least live.*

In a letter to Conrad, Archbishop of Mayence, our Saint speaks of the sharpness of this fresh trial of the suspension of his legatine powers :—

> At present the King of England is causing my suspension to be cried through the streets of both kingdoms, and, in witness of my overthrow, is exhibiting the Apostolic Letters to make me odious and wearisome in the sight of men. He boasts that the term granted him lasts till he pleases to receive me into favour, which, if he is allowed, he will put off till the Greek Kalends, *i.e.* for ever.

It was on the 9th of October, 1166, that the Holy Father had appointed S. Thomas his Legate over England; and in May, 1168, these powers had been suspended until the following Lent, when they were to be restored if the King did not come to terms earlier.

* Froude, p. 360.

At the period of which we are about to speak, S. Thomas's suspension was ended, and the King felt that the ecclesiastical sword was again in his opponent's hands, and hung over his head by a single hair. Letters actually empowering S. Thomas to lay Henry's kingdom under an interdict had been forwarded to the Saint in case of the King's persisting longer in his refusal to submit to terms. Thus it seems to have been a design to get S. Thomas once more into his power, and no real desire for a reconciliation with one whom he had come to regard with the bitterest hatred, which was the cause of his interview and pretended reconciliation with the Saint at Freitval.*

* That Henry had some sinister design in this last conference can hardly be doubted by those who read the account of it. The Archbishop's party were quite surprised at this sudden desire for peace on the part of a monarch who had been so inexorable for nearly seven

It would take us far beyond the limits of this sketch, already longer than we had proposed, were we to enter into the interesting accounts of these interviews between Henry and his exile, or the struggles of the Archbishop to bring those of his suffragans who so shamefully and unnaturally opposed him, back to their duty. Roger de Pont l'Evêque, Archbishop of York, and the Bishops of London and Salisbury, were amongst the foremost of those who tried their uttermost

years, and plainly the Archbishop himself was filled with misgivings after the interview was over. One of his historians tells us that some one in the King's interest had hinted to Henry that it was a mistake to keep the Archbishop out of the country, "as he would be far better in than out." But first, continues the historian, he caused his son to be crowned with despatch, on account of a certain result which might possibly take place; so that if a crime were committed the kingdom could not be punished on *his* account, seeing that he would no longer be King of it.

to ruin the Saint, both at Rome and with the King, and who rebelled most openly against his authority; and of these the Bishop of London was, as we have seen, the most prominent throughout the whole contest.

The coronation of the young Prince Henry by the Archbishop of York, at the King's command, had put the finishing stroke to the series of contumacious acts of these bishops, whose whole course had been insult and disobedience to their spiritual chief. For the coronation of the King of England was one of the undoubted prerogatives of the See of Canterbury; and when S. Thomas, who saw what was about to happen, sent letters obtained from Rome forbidding any one but the Archbishop of Canterbury to perform the ceremony, they were utterly disregarded by the Archbishop of York and the Bishop of London, to whom they were delivered.

It was now six long, weary years that S. Thomas had passed in exile, and endured, in addition to all his other trials, that hope long deferred which maketh the heart sick. The last interview with the King near the Castle of Freitval, when King Henry made a show of reconciliation and restitution, decided S. Thomas to return to his desolate See and Church.

Many were the misgivings of the Saint's friends at his resolution of returning into the power of a king who had shown himself so wily, so treacherous, and so implacable a foe. None of them believed in Henry's seeming reconciliation, and the King himself still refused to give the Saint the kiss of peace at mass. When S. Thomas wrote to Rome to inform the Pope and his court of the apparent peace of Freitval, Cardinal Albert observed: "The Ethiopian does not easily change his skin, or the leopard his spots." The Saint himself, on going to say farewell to his kind friend the King of France, said, "We are going to England to play at heads." "So it seems to me," replied the King; and then he urged the Saint never to trust himself in King Henry's dominions so long as that prince refused to give him the kiss of peace. "Remain," he said; "and, as long as King Louis lives, the wine, the food, and the wealth of France shall never fail you." But S. Thomas knew that his Master's Will was otherwise, and that his hour was at hand. He replied, with tears, to his generous friend, "God's Will be done;" and, with a like emotion on the part of the King of France, they parted. To the Bishop of Paris our Saint also spoke prophetically of the event of his return. "I am going to England," he said, "to die." He took leave of King Henry, saying that his heart warned him that the King would never see him alive again.

The King's intention seems to have been clear enough to his ministers and to the barons of his court. From the varied evidence on the subject, it seems manifest that the speech of the King which caused the final catastrophe was rather the expression of impatience at the delay of those who knew his wishes, in executing them, than any sudden ebullition of anger which conveyed no grave intention, as some historians have intimated. Reginald de Warenne told the canons of the Southwark Chapter, who were great friends of his, that he hoped they would pray for him, for that he had great need of it. Soon, he said, something would be done in England such as had never before been heard of, but that it was against his (De Warenne's) will, he not being his own master.

In concluding his affairs, to return to his diocese, S. Thomas wrote two letters, one to the Pope, and another to the King of England. In the former he employs all his influence with the Holy Father to induce him to use the weapons of the Church with such gentleness and forbearance towards her adversaries as may leave no plea for breaking the supposed peace: "That he [the Pope] should write to the King tenderly, and explain how that the Lord hath established the Apostolical See," &c. He entreated the Holy Father that the Bishop of London's sedition—not to call it schism—might be pardoned, as well as the Bishop of Salisbury's, and the excommunication of the other bishops (excepting the Archbishop of York) left to his (S. Thomas's) discretion; promising to use the same with a view to God's honour and the Pope's. In all which we see how beautifully the Saint mingled forbearance, tenderness, and compassion towards his enemies with his ardent zeal and enthusiasm for the cause and honour of God.*

His letter to the King, while evincing the same spirit, shows what real grounds he had for mistrusting that deceitful and treacherous monarch.†

---

* Note from Canon Morris, p. 294.—It subsequently transpired that one of the serjeants of the King's court had with his own hands sealed the letters which were sent to England to command the death of the Archbishop; Nigel de Sacville having written them. And he added that he had confessed this to an English bishop and asked for a penance; but the bishop had said: "What for? You did your lord's command." And, as if he had done no harm, enjoined him nothing.

† Froude, p. 525.

Christ, the Inspector of hearts, knoweth with what sincere intentions we made peace with you, trusting to a like good faith on your Highness's part towards ourselves. For what less, my lord, could we expect after those arguments and words of consolation which your Highness's benignity addressed to us? Your letters, also, to our lord the King, your son, touching the restitution to us and ours of the possessions which we held before our departure, what other profession did they make but that of benevolence and peace? But now, more to your own dishonour than to our disadvantage (God knoweth how sincerely we think so), manifestations are being made the very opposite of sincerity and good faith. For the councillors of our lord the King, your son (who these are, and how far they are to be trusted is for your lordship to inquire), have now, on pretence of summoning Randolph (de Broc), put off the making restitution. The Church, your honour, and your soul, must suffer from such proceedings, unless you speedily correct them. Meantime the said Randolph violently outrages the property of the Church, collects our stores into the Castle of Saltwode, and, as we have been informed by those who can prove it, has in the hearing of many boasted that we shall not long enjoy our peace, "for that before we have eaten a loaf of bread in England he will take away our life."

Your Highness knows that voluntarily to overlook a wrong is to participate in the guilt. Yet is this Ran dolph plainly relying on your countenance and authority, for how else could he venture so far? What was the answer he returned to your son's letters? We leave this for your discretion to reflect upon when you are informed of it.

Forasmuch, however, as there are plain indications that, through hatred of our person, the Mother of the British Churches is in danger of perishing, we, in order to save her from this fate, are prepared, God willing, to surrender our life into the hands of Randolph and his accomplices in persecution; yea, and to die a thousand deaths for Christ's sake, if His grace enable us.

I had intended, my lord, ere now, to have returned to you; but the necessities of the afflicted Church draw me to her side. With your favour and permission, I purpose returning to her—perhaps, unless your timely pity ordain it otherwise, to die for her.

Yours, whether we live or die, now and ever in the Lord.

John of Salisbury also wrote a letter to his friend, the Abbot of S. Remy,[*] showing too plainly the hollow character of Henry's seeming reconciliation, and the ruinous condition of the Archbishop's possessions. We

[*] Froude, p. 527.

trust we shall be forgiven for inserting it at full length, as a beautiful specimen of the devoted loyalty of S. Thomas's friends, and the pure and fervent faith and piety of many of the devout priests and others of that period :—

JOHN OF SALISBURY TO PETER, ABBOT OF S. REMY.

You might well accuse my delay if I had not necessity to excuse it. I ought, when I first set foot in England, to have sent back a messenger to certify your goodness of the state of your children. Yet so entirely new and strange was the whole face of affairs which met me on leaving the vessel that my own utter uncertainty ill qualified me for certifying another.

Three days before I landed, a mark had been set on all the effects of his Lordship of Canterbury ; and his proctors had been excluded from all share in administering them. Also an edict had been published in all the ports, forbidding, under penalty of exile and proscription, that any of our party should leave England.

Such has been the pious circumspection of the King's officers that the Archbishop and his friends, on their return from exile, have little to find except empty and dismantled houses, dilapidated barns, and naked threshing-floors. This is their consolation for their long proscription, the amends made them for the sacrilege of which they have been the victims. And, whereas our peace had been made on the feast of S. Magdalen, and our most serene lord the King had instructed his son, by his letters patent, that all things were to be restored to the Archbishop and his, entire as they had been before he left England, yet all the revenues which will become due up to Christmas have been already seized in the King's name. Moreover, many churches and possessions which by right and by the terms of our covenant should have been restored to the See of Canterbury are still in the occupation of laymen, under State authority. I, among others, have been deprived of a church which brought my predecessor 40 marks a year.

It happened that I landed three days before the octave of S. Martin; on the octave a synod was to be held at Canterbury, in which I had to supply the vacant place of the Archbishop; so when I found, contrary to my hopes and expectations, and to the King's promises, that the Archbishop's restoration was altogether despaired of, and that I myself was in a manner under arrest, I set out for Canterbury with as cheerful a countenance and as quiet a mind as I could summon. There I was received, both by clergy and people, with great honour and, as it were, an angel of the Lord.

From my return the faithful seemed to have conceived better hopes, as they felt sure that the Archbishop would never have sent me forward unless he was himself on the point to follow. When the synod was concluded I set out to present myself before the young King. He received me graciously enough; but those about him intimated that all was not safe: they suspected that peace had not been made with us in sincerity, and that the rancour which had been nominally softened was in reality more firmly fixed than ever. I myself saw too many signs of this, but conducted myself as if all was going on according to my wishes. From hence I made my way in all haste to my mother: she was languishing on another year, and, since she saw me, is now expecting the day of the Lord with joy. I commend her earnestly to your prayers, and to those of the Saints with whom you dwell. She had received an answer from the Spirit that she should not taste death till she had seen me and my brother return from exile.

Such was the state of things on the eve of the Saint's return to Canterbury after his long exile. Pope Alexander meanwhile had not entirely conceded to S. Thomas's tenderness towards his foes all for which it had pleaded. The length of the struggle, the bitterness and animosity of the King and those of the clergy who sided with him, demonstrated more and more forcibly to the Roman Court the spirit by which they were animated, and the hopelessness of coming to terms with them. On the other hand, the ever-increasing saintliness of the Archbishop, his deep and prolonged sufferings, and the exalted dignity, firmness, and greatness of soul with which he placed his cause in the hands of his Lord, and prepared to return and abide the result, was evidence to the Pope that the cause of the Church must be strengthened in his person if it were to prevail. Alexander, therefore, forwarded to S. Thomas letters suspending the Archbishop of York and the other bishops (excepting Exeter) who were participators in the coronation of the young King, and excommunicating the Bishops of London and Salisbury. These were intrusted by the Primate to faithful messengers, and sent on to England before him. The one for the Archbishop of York was given to a nun named Idonea to deliver, who, with the devotion shown by her sex even from the times of the Apostles, fulfilled a mission fraught with danger for the love of God and veneration for His servant.

These three bishops, having had intimation of the arms which the Primate was bringing against them, repaired to the coast with Randulph de Broc and a party of his soldiers, intending to seize the Primate and take the letters of excommunication from him by force. Some have even said that they proposed to countenance his massacre by the soldiers. Instead of meeting S. Thomas, however, they met his messengers, who thus caught them in their own snare, and served the letters of excommunication upon them.

The Archbishop of Canterbury and Primate of England—for now that he is about to return to his Church we must give him his full titles—embarked from Wytsand or Ouessant, in the territory of Boulogne, on a Tuesday, that day of the week which had been marked by all the chief events of his life, the 1st of December, 1170. He set out, accompanied by—or rather, as Lingard says, in the custody of—one of the chiefs of his old enemies, John of Oxford, whom the King sent as his delegate, and by his own followers. As they stood on the sea-shore, the sea and sky calm and serene and the ship in readiness, the Archbishop paused and gazed at the scene before him. Perhaps, his soul, permitted by his Lord so clear a vision of his approaching martyrdom, was lifting itself to that Lord whence came his help for strength to walk forward to meet the bloody death which awaited him. Some of his clergy and co-exiles said, with the natural and passionate longing for their native land, so long sighed for and now almost in view before them: " My lord, look, we can see England! Why do you hesitate, and, gazing like Moses upon the land of promise, behold, yet enter it not?" The Archbishop turned to them: "You hasten now," he said. "Not forty days hence, and you will rather be in any corner of the earth than in England."

The Primate and his suite were pursued with warnings to the very water's edge. The Earl of Boulogne sent to them a messenger: "Beware," he said to the Archbishop; "the ports are beset with men who seek your life; who, as soon as you leave the vessel, will either murder you or deprive you of your liberty." But the Archbishop replied: "Did you tell me I were to be torn limb from limb,

I would not regard it; for I am resolved that nothing shall hinder my return. Seven years are long enough for a pastor to have been absent from the Lord's sorrowing flock; I will only ask my friends (and a *last* request *should* be attended to) that, if I cannot return to my Church alive, they will carry me into it dead." The crew of an English vessel almost at the same time urged the Archbishop's followers not to go forward into England, where they declared destruction awaited them, and spoke of the excitement caused by the recent suspensions. But the Archbishop's resolution was fixed. "In England I am resolved to be," he said; "I am aware of the consequences."

For greater security, and not to neglect all wise human precautions, the Archbishop landed at Sandwich, which was one of his own ports. His return was the signal for general joy. At Sandwich the people watched for his vessel; and when they saw the Archiepiscopal cross, which marked it from the others, they rushed into the water to receive him. The road to Canterbury was thronged with people, especially the poor, whose friend he had ever so truly been, invoking the blessing of Heaven upon him —" Blessed is he who cometh in the name of the Lord;" and the clergy, with crucifixes before them, led out their parishioners to meet him. At Canterbury the enthusiasm increased. The inhabitants decked out the cathedral, rang the bells, and, arraying themselves in silks and holiday dresses, prepared a public entertainment. " The churches," says Fitzstephen, "resounded with chants and anthems, and the halls with trumpets, and the rejoicing was general."

The triumph of the Archbishop was thus

far complete. While abroad in exile, his noble conduct and long suffering for the cause of God had drawn down the blessings of the French people as he passed along the roads, after meeting his persecutor; and now he was amongst his own countrymen, by whom he had ever been beloved, and who had come to regard him as a saint and confessor for their Church and her rights.

The Primate went straight to his cathedral, and walked up to the episcopal throne, receiving there the religious to the kiss of peace. His face was remarked to shine with a supernatural splendour, and the people all round him wept with joy. His faithful Herbert said to him: "My lord, we do not now mind when you may have to leave the world, for the Church, Christ's Spouse, has this day conquered in you." To which words the Archbishop only replied by looking at his friend.

The Saint preached in the chapter-house an impressive sermon, on a text most suitable indeed to his own circumstances: "We have here no abiding city, but seek one to come."

Meantime the suspended prelates sent their chaplains with the soldiers to the Primate to desire absolution from the censures; saying that he had not come in peace, but in sword and in fire, trampling on his fellow-bishops, and making them as the sole of his feet, uncited, unheard, unjudged; that his suffragans had gone to sea to meet him, but that they had unexpectedly found themselves dressed in certain black garments of which, if his lordship pleased, they must be ridded before they should present themselves. In his answer he said that "there was no true peace except to men of good will: Jerusalem, abounding in luxury and self-indulgence, said to herself, It is peace; but the Lord wept over it, because the vengeance of God hung over it and was hid from its eyes." Their sentence, he reminded them, was passed by the Pope, nor was it for them to call in question his Holiness's acts. On their pressing him very earnestly, however, for the absolution, S. Thomas, for the sake of peace, promised to accept their oath to obey the judgment of the Pope, and to do what he could for them after consulting the King and the other bishops, subject always to the Pope's approbation. But the bishops rejected this offer as an insult to the Crown, and sent their emissaries on to the King on the Continent to take further measures of rebellious opposition.

After about a week passed in his diocesan

city, S. Thomas sent messengers to the young King to announce his intention of waiting upon him. He had brought over with him for this prince a present of three magnificent horses, with embroidered trappings ornamented with flowers, "for he regarded him with great kindness," says the old historian,* "having brought him up as a boy."

On his way to London the Bishop of Rochester, brother of the late Archbishop Theobald, met him with a procession of his clergy; and as he entered the City another procession conducted him to the Church of S. Mary's, Southwark. The poor scholars and clerics of London went out to meet him, and, while they made the air resound with the Te Deum, the people shed tears of joy.

* Fitzstephen.

S. Thomas bowed his head in gratitude, scattering alms around. The Southwark canons received him at the door of S. Mary's, singing the Benedictus, and he was lodged in the Bishop of Winchester's palace. But in the midst of these rejoicings a crazy woman named Matilda repeatedly cried out, "Archbishop, beware of the knife!"

The next day S. Thomas received a peremptory message from the young King, ordering him back at once to Canterbury. He asked in vain for an explanation, but was excluded from the royal presence. This fresh blow from his former youthful friend and pupil seems to have struck the Saint's heart, so tender in its friendships, affections, and memories, and to have filled him with the worst forebodings. For we find him on the 13th of December, the feast of S. Lucy, at his manor of Harrow, receiving a visit from his friend the Abbot of S. Alban's, for whom he had sent, saying that never had he so much needed consolation as then. When he had detailed the events of the last sad years of exile, the Abbot said to him, "By God's grace, that is now all happily ended;" but the Saint replied, sighing, and pressing the Abbot's hand: "My friend, my friend, I will tell you my case as to another self. Things are very different with me to what men think. New persecutions are beginning. The King and his son, who is my only hope, are devising fresh injuries." "How can this be, holy father?" said the Abbot. The Saint looked up to Heaven, and, with a deep sigh, he added, "Well enough, well enough I know to what matters are tending." They parted, the Saint enjoining the Abbot to invoke for him his patron, S. Thomas Apostle and Martyr.

Although S. Thomas in returning to Canterbury was only accompanied by five soldiers, a guard absolutely necessary in those times against marauders, it was reported to King Henry that he was marching about England with a large army in helmets and coats of mail, besieging towns and intending to drive the young King out of the country. On arriving at Canterbury he dismissed his escort.

On his road home, at Wrotham, he fell in with a poor priest named William, who, begging a private audience, said that he had brought the Archbishop some relics of S. Lawrence, S. Vincent, and S. Cecilia, as S. Lawrence had told him to do in a vision. S. Thomas asked him how he knew that they were the relics of those Saints. The priest replied: "My lord, in my vision I asked S. Lawrence for some sign ; for I said that otherwise you would not believe me. And S. Lawrence told me that you lately put your hand into your breast and found the hair shirt torn which you wear next your skin, and, while you were deliberating whether you should have it repaired or a new one made, you put your hand in again and found it whole." The Saint, on hearing this, charged the priest, in virtue of obedience, to tell no one as long as he (S. Thomas) lived. The priest promised, and begged of his patron to think of him, who was a poor man serving in another man's church. One of the last recorded acts of the Saint's life was to make out a deed giving this poor cleric the chapel of Pensehurst, and subjoining an anathema to any one who dared to deprive him of it.

Meantime the infamous family of the de Brocs neglected no opportunity of insulting and injuring the Primate and his dependents. From the Castle of Saltwode, which they had robbed from his See, they cut off the Archbishop's stores as they arrived by sea, killed the deer in his chase, stole his dogs, and on Christmas-eve Robert de Broc, an apostate monk, waylaid a train of the Archbishop's pack-horses, and cut off the tail of one of them as a special insult.

The letter of John of Salisbury to the Abbot of S. Remy, which we have already quoted, describes the grievous position of the Saint and his friends at this period. "No way seems now open for our consolation and safety," he says, "unless the prayers of yourself and the Saints can deliver us from the snares of those who would wipe us utterly away from the earth; yet, though the persecution is most grievous, and few among the rich and honourable come near the Archbishop, he himself with the dignity of a bishop does justice for all that come near to him, laying aside all consideration of persons." On Christmas-night, the Archbishop sang the Gospel of the Nativity after Matins, as is still the usage of the Benedictine order, and celebrated the midnight Mass himself. He sang the High Mass on Christmas-day and preached on the text, "On earth peace to men of good will." His eloquence and enthusiasm increased with the occasion, and reached its height as he spoke of the Holy Fathers of the Church of Canterbury, the confessors who were there. "One Archbishop and Martyr they had had already," he said— "S. Elphege, murdered by the Danes; it was possible they might have another soon." The tears burst from his eyes; his sobs interrupted his words, and his emotion arose to anguish. The soul which had toiled, and suffered, and agonized for His sake was likened to its Lord at last; it was the martyrdom of the spirit, the cry of a heart crucified and broken with the love of God.

The people around him wept and groaned in passionate sorrow. "Father," they cried, "why do you desert us so soon? To whom do you leave us desolate?" Putting a strong restraint on his tears, the Saint with clear and authoritative voice pronounced excommunication against Robert de Broc, as he had forewarned that obstinate offender, whom he had summoned to do penance, and who had returned for answer that if he were excommunicate he would act as such. In the same sentence were included the usurpers of S. Thomas's two churches of Harrow and Thierlwood.

On the two following feasts, S. Stephen

and S. John, the Saint sang Mass, and on the latter day S. Thomas received a letter warning him of his impending fate. One of the citizens of Canterbury also, known to S. Thomas, warned him that the murderers had landed in England, and were advancing for his destruction. But the Saint, who knew already that the hour of his martyrdom was approaching, only replied with tears: "I know, my son, that I shall die a violent death; but they will not kill me outside my church." On the feast of S. Stephen, the Saint sent off his cross-bearer, Alexander, and another of his suite to bear a letter to the Holy Father, and his chaplain Herbert to the King and some of his friends in France. It was the last letter he ever wrote to the Pope. After describing his return to his diocese, the grievous position he found himself in, and the dangers which surrounded him, he mentions the departure of the three bishops to King Henry's court in France for their uncanonical purposes, on that evil expedition which was in fact the moving cause of his martyrdom. These persons, he said, dreaded nothing so much as the peace of the Church, lest its discipline should interfere with their irregularities. The letter ends, " May your Holiness fare well for ever, dearest father."

The excommunicated bishops crossed the sea, and repaired to the King at his palace of Bur, near Bayeux, and there detailed to him, with many exaggerations and false statements, their tale of grievances; not forgetting to enlarge on the Archbishop's *armed progresses*, as they called the peaceful processions of his clergy. Although Henry appears to have affected to authorize S.

Thomas to punish the injuries to his Church, and already knew of the excommunications, he pretended to be ignorant of them. " By God's eyes," said the King, " if all who were concerned in my son's coronation are to be excommunicated, I will be excommunicated too." He then asked what they would advise him to do? Roger of York replied: " It is not for us to advise your Highness, your barons will do that;" " but," added one of them, " My lord, while Thomas lives you will not have peace or quiet, or see another good day." Upon this the King burst into one of his violent fits of rage; his eyes flashed fire, and his whole face was distorted, resembling the unhappy spirit that animated it. " What slothful wretches have I maintained in my court,".he exclaimed ; " not one will deliver me from this low-born cleric." And thus saying, he left the council-chamber.

Four barons, continues the old chronicle, —Reginald Fitzurse, William de Traci, Hugh de Moreville, and Richard de Bryto — left the court, and crossed the Channel from different ports, and, by the guidance of the devil, the ancient enemy of all good, assembled all at the same hour at Saltwode, the castle of the de Brocs. The King called a council of his barons, whose observations and advice showed them to have been proper courtiers to such a monarch.

Engelgere de Bohun,* an excommunicate, said of the Saint, "I do not know what you are to do with such a fellow, except you

---

* In an old history of the Isle of Wight there is mention of some large gifts of lands made by " Engel de Bohun " to the richly-endowed Abbey of Quarr, near Ryde, no long time after the murder of S. Thomas. The fact would seem to show that this noble had afterwards desired to do penance for his persecution of the Church of God in the person of His Saint.

bind him with a wicker rope, and hang him on a cross." William Malvoisin observed that he had heard, when at Rome, that a certain Pope had been killed on account of his intolerable haughtiness and insolence.

The King then sent some knights after those who had left, as it was reported, to seize the Archbishop. The ports were all guarded, and orders sent for household troops to repair privately to Canterbury.

On the Monday, the feast of the Holy Innocents, the four murderers held their council at Saltwode; and on Tuesday, with their retainers, and the whole de Broc family, and soldiers gathered from the neighbouring castles, they rode forward to Canterbury.

Meantime, our Saint had been preparing himself with fervent devotion for the death which he knew was rapidly coming upon him. He had recited Matins with his clerics and monks at midnight of the Holy Innocents; and when they were finished, he opened a window and stood for a long time in silence looking out into the night. Then, as if human nature seemed to arise for a moment and urge him to avoid a bloody death, he suddenly turned and asked those near him what time it was, and whether it would be possible to reach Sandwich before daybreak? They replied that a much further distance might be gained, as it was yet quite early, and that place was but seven miles off. If, however, any such power of the flesh oppressed the spirit, it was but for a moment; for he quickly murmured to himself, "God's will be done in me! Thomas will wait for whatever God has in store for him in the church over which he presides."

The Tuesday dawned, the 29th of December, 1170—that day which was to be honoured throughout Christendom in future ages as sacred to one of the Church's greatest saints and martyrs. S. Thomas assisted at the Cathedral Mass, and remained in spiritual conference for two hours in the chapter-house with two of the monks most noted for their piety. He made his confession with deepest marks of contrition, and received the discipline three times on that day of preparation for joining the saints in heaven; and when afterwards his cheerfulness at table was remarked upon by one of his religious, he replied: "A man must be cheerful who is going to his Master."

The Archbishop and his monks and clerics had dined, and grace having been chanted, they retired into the Archbishop's room, where he sat upon the bed, with his friends reclining around him at his feet. There seem to have been present John of

Salisbury, William Fitzstephen, Robert Prior of Merton, Edward Grim, a young cleric from Cambridge, and several religious. The servants and attendants were still at dinner in the hall, as was the custom after their superiors had left, and the doors were yet open which admitted the crowd of poor daily relieved from the Saint's table, when the four knights, with an attendant archer, entered the hall. They rejected the offers of refreshment made to them by the Saint's attendants, and passed on to the foot of the staircase which led to the Archbishop's room. There they met his Seneschal, William Fitznigel, who recognized them as courtiers, and at their request led the way to the room in which the Saint and his friends were. "My lord," he said, "here are four knights from the King wishing to speak with you." "Let them come in,"

S. Thomas replied, continuing his conversation with the religious next him, and on whose shoulder he was leaning, without looking towards his sudden guests. They gave no attention to the Archbishop, but sat down amongst the clerics at his feet, with Radulf, their archer, behind them.

S. Thomas then turned round and saluted William de Traci by name. Of this salutation, however, the knights took no notice, but gazed on each other in silence; until at length Fitzurse said scornfully, "God help you!" The colour rushed into the Saint's face; but he kept silence, while the knights still glared fiercely at him and at each other. Fitzurse continued, "We have commands for you from the King over the water; say if you will hear them privately or in the hearing of all." "As you wish," replied S. Thomas. "No; as you wish," said

Fitzurse. Finally, the room being cleared, Fitzurse began to speak about the absolution of the bishops; when the Saint ordered the clergy to return, saying that these things ought not to be told in secret.

The murderers afterwards confessed that during the few moments they were then left alone with the Archbishop, they had thought of killing him with his archiepiscopal cross, no other weapon being at hand.

On the return of the clerics, S. Thomas said, "Now, you may tell your lord's will in their presence." Fitzurse then said, as the Archbishop had chosen to make these things public instead of private, he would satisfy him and tell the matters before all present. He then represented that the King said that he had made peace in good faith, but that the Archbishop had violated his engagements, gone about Henry's kingdom with armed bands, and excommunicated the Archbishop of York and others for crowning the young king; and that the King called upon him to wait upon his son at Winton, and make amends for his treason and swear fealty, and further ordered him to absolve the bishops. The Archbishop asked, "What treason? and for what was he to swear fealty?" He said that he had already tried to see the young king and had been refused; that he was ready to do fealty for his barony, which he held of the King; but that as to the excommunications and suspensions, they were done by the Pope; and he added, that although he was not sorry that the offence against his Church had been punished, he had already offered to absolve his suffragans, the Bishops of London and Salisbury, on their submission and oath to obey the judgment of the Pope, but that they had refused.

And as to his treason, he said he would, far from uncrowning the young king, rejoice to give him three crowns and more dominions. Fitzurse then spoke yet more insolently; the Archbishop, he said, was accusing the King of deepest treachery in acquiescing in the punishment of bishops who had but obeyed his orders. "Yours is an awful crime," he said, "in feigning such treachery of our lord the King." "Reginald, Reginald," said the Saint, "I do not accuse the King of treachery. Our reconciliation was not so secretly done; but I appeal to the archbishops, bishops, men of rank, religious, and more than five hundred knights who were there and heard it, and yourself, Sir Reginald, who were present." Fitzurse swore that he was not present. The Saint replied, "God knows it, for I am certain that I saw you there." The knights then became more excited: they swore by God's wounds that they had borne with him too long, and, as the King's liegemen, would bear with him no longer; and then, as if resolved to find some more distinct pretext for their meditated violence, they asked him from whom he held his Archbishopric. The Archbishop replied, "Its spiritualities from God and my lord the Pope, and its temporalities from the King." "Own," said they, "that you have it all from the King." S. Thomas replied, "By no means; for we are commanded to render unto Cæsar the things that are Cæsar's, and unto God the things that are God's." Upon this they gnashed upon him with their teeth. He added that since he came to England under the King's safe-conduct, he had been threatened, insulted, and injured, which was hard measure. De Moreville here asked why, if injured, he had not complained to the King, instead of excommunicating the offenders on his own authority. To which he replied, "Hugh, how you lift up your head! If the rights of the Church are injured, I shall wait for no man's leave to do justice."

Upon this the knights cast off all restraint; they glared upon the Saint like wild beasts, leapt upon their feet, twisted their long gloves wildly, threw up their arms, and gnashed their teeth with fury. "Threats! threats!" they said; "is he going to excommunicate us all? God be merciful to us; he shall not do it; he has excommunicated too many already!"

The Archbishop turned to them with dignity: "My lords," he said, "you threaten me in vain. If all the swords in England were pointed at me, your terrors could not move me from the observance of God's justice and allegiance to our Lord the Pope. I know that you have come here to kill me, but I make God my shield. Foot to foot you will find me in the battle of the Lord. I fled from my duty once, but will do so no more for ever. Moreover," he added, " I wonder the more at your conduct, considering what there is between you and me." This was in allusion to the fealty which Fitzurse, Traci, and Moreville had sworn to him when Chancellor. They shouted, "There is nothing between us against the King; we can do no more than threaten the Archbishop—let us go."

A number of the Archbishop's household, alarmed at the loud conversation, were now collected, both clerics and men-at-arms; to whom Fitzurse turned, and charged them as the King's liegemen, to keep "this man" in safe custody. The Archbishop said that would be easy, for he should not go away. "I shall not fly," he said, "for the King or any living man;" and, following the knights to the door, he struck his hand on the very spot of his death-wound, saying, "Here, here you will find me."

John of Salisbury now reproached him with following the knights to the door, which he said had made them more angry; that he should rather have called his Council and given them a milder answer. S. Thomas replied that counsel was already taken, and he knew what he ought to do. "We must all die," he said, "and the fear of men must not turn us from justice. I am more ready to die," he added, "for God and the liberty of His Church, than they are to inflict death upon me."

The knights, who had entered the Archbishop's room with their capes and tunics on over their coats of mail, had gone out to take these garments off, and arm themselves for their deed of violence. Some of the Archbishop's people and others, who saw this and had heard the soldiers ordered to the palace, rushed into the Saint's presence, exclaiming, "My lord, they are arming." But they could not disturb the Saint, who said calmly, "Let them arm." The clerics and religious, however, desiring that he should take sanctuary, urged him to go into the church. After withstanding for a little what he called the timidity of the monks, he consented to go and assist at vespers, which had begun. Desiring, therefore, his cross to be borne before him, he walked down the long passages and cloisters into the cathedral, calming by his self-possession the panic fears of his companions.

The monks in choir, disturbed and thrown

into confusion by the alarm of some of those who had rushed forward into the church in terror, began some to pray, and some to fly towards the Archbishop as he entered, who they almost feared was already killed. He desired them to return and proceed with the office. But when they would have closed the doors of the cathedral, he commanded them to be opened, saying, " A church must not be closed as a fortress. Suffer all that will to enter the house of God."

Meanwhile, the murderers had sought the Archbishop in his palace; and not finding him, they marched towards the cathedral, breaking down such doors or barriers as intercepted their course. It was nearly five o'clock in the evening, in the very depth of winter, and the days at their shortest. The clerics who surrounded the Archbishop, after urging him to avail himself of the twilight and seek concealment in the many accessible hiding-places in the cathedral, fled away for this purpose themselves, all except Edward Grim. But the true shepherd giveth his life for his sheep, and the Archbishop refused to fly. "Leave hold of me," said he to his terrified followers, "and go away; there is nothing for you to do here; let God dispose of me as He will."

The Saint and his companions had reached the north transept of the cathedral which enclosed altars to our Lady, to S. Blaise, martyr, and to S. Benedict. Here the murderers overtook them, and cried out, "Where is Thomas, traitor to the King?" To this the Saint made no reply. Fitzurse then said, "Where is the Archbishop?" S. Thomas turned, and advanced, replying, "Here I am, the Archbishop, but no traitor." Then one of them struck him between the shoulders with the flat of his sword. " Fly," said he, " or you are a dead man." The Saint replied, " I will not fly." " Absolve the bishops whom you have excommunicated!" they cried. He answered, " I will do nothing more than I have already said and done." S. Thomas then said to Fitzurse, " Reginald, I have done you many favours, do you come against me in arms?" "You shall know it," replied Fitzurse; "are you not a traitor?" S. Thomas replied, "I do not fear your threats, for I am prepared to die for God; but I charge you by His authority that you touch none of mine." They then tried to drag him out of the church; but he resisted, and stood firm, Edward Grim aiding him; and he exerting his strength, nearly flung Fitzurse on the pavement, while he pronounced judgment upon him for the immorality of his life.

"Promoter of wickedness," he said, "you are my man, and shall not touch me; you owe me fealty and submission." "I owe you neither," said the knight, "contrary to my fealty to the King."

Fitzurse then pressed upon him. "Ferez! ferez!" he said (strike, strike), and waved his sword for the first blow. The Saint saw it coming, joined his hands, and covered his eyes with them, bowing his head. "I commend myself to God, Holy Mary, S. Denys, and S. Elphege," he said. The blow fell, and Edward Grim, raising his arm to intercept it, nearly lost his limb, while the Saint's head was smitten on the tonsure. He wiped away the blood which was streaming from his brow, giving thanks to God, and saying, "Into Thy hands, O Lord, I commend my spirit." A second blow made him fall on his knees, and then on his face, his hands still joined, and stretched out to God, before the altar of S. Benedict. There he breathed out his last words, "For the name of Jesus and the defence of the Church I am ready to die." Even thus he was struck again by the sword of Richard de Bryto with such violence that the sword broke on the pavement. This wretched nobleman added as he dealt the blow, "Take that for the love of my lord William, the King's brother," alluding to an iniquitous marriage between the latter and the Countess de Warenne, which S. Thomas had prevented. Another of his murderers put his foot on the Saint's neck, and drew out his brains with his sword's point. "Let us go," said he, "the traitor is dead; he will rise no more." They then all marched from the church, shouting as before, "Reaux! Reaux!" (king's men! king's men!)

The corpse of the martyr lay composed and graceful even in death, as of one prostrate in prayer.

His clerics and religious, hearing the clamour cease, came forth from the different parts of the church, and gathered together around the corpse. Weeping with anguish and grief, they placed it on a bier, and then Father Robert of Merton, his confessor, drew aside his vest, and showed his monks the fearful hair shirt which this servant of God had worn to scourge and crucify the flesh, while the spirit had been enduring so long a martyrdom for the cause of his Heavenly Master; at the sight of which they all knelt down, and calling him God's glorious Saint and Martyr, invoked his prayers.

As is usually the case at the death of Saints, proofs of his sanctity, unsuspected during his life, came to light. Not only were the marks of the severe discipline he took visible on his body, but his hair shirt, itself unknown to those about him, was filled with vermin, which must have caused constant and terrible suffering to his skin.

It was the Divine Will, too, that the miracles which were wrought by his relics, and on the places that his body had touched, should follow his martyrdom with special promptitude, so as to leave no time to doubt the fact of the sanctity of him who had died for his Lord. And the miracles occurred in such numbers, and with such perfect evidence, as to silence even the mouths of his enemies, who would fain have concealed or thrown discredit upon them.

Much might now be added to show that there was no real evidence of repentance on the part of King Henry for the crime in which he had so large a share; but our space warns us to be brief.

In drawing to a close this sketch of the Saint which we have attempted, it may be well to say a few words on the early friendship between S. Thomas and King Henry, which ended in such complete estrangement. It has not unfrequently excited the surprise of those who have read their history, that two men, bound together apparently by ties of such close friendship and affection, and who pursued, as it appears, for so many years the same ends, should so suddenly separate, and each embrace a course which led to such entire opposition, and, on the King's part, to such deep hatred. Yet to any one who follows their career with the eye of faith, the whole history of these two men is but the natural development and contrast of one who was ever at heart the disciple of Christ, and another who was with equal sincerity the votary of the world. Both of them were men of great abilities, prompt, vigorous, and energetic in action; both naturally of passionate temperament and strong feelings; both also had high and ambitious views and great aims. With these similarities in their natural character, it was surely not wonderful that in the beginning of their intimacy, and while the King was yet young, they should understand each other better than those about them; that the King should value a man so fitted to do justice to the grandeur of his ideas, and that the Chancellor should feel an affection and devotion to a sovereign so well able to appreciate his abilities. And the generous soul of S. Thomas,—which seemed to take pleasure in the splendour by which he was surrounded, more because it enhanced his master's honour than for its worth to himself,—was peculiarly attractive to Henry's pride. "For this monarch," says Lingard, "was careful that his favourites should owe everything to himself, and gloried in the parade of their power and opulence, because they were of his own creation." When, however, the circumstances of their lives changed, and called forth those latent principles which were deep in the hearts of both, they gradually diverged. The King followed his ambition, and making that his leading motive of action, threw his great abilities into obtaining all which that led him to seek, without any check to those qualities of pride, passion, and violence which were his natural characteristics; and, pursuing his worldly aim with as much determination as his Primate pursued the cause of God, he not unnaturally came to hate the man who was the one obstacle to all his wishes.

But in the case of the Primate, under the shadow of the crucifix which was impressed on his heart amidst all his pomp, his high abilities and energetic temperament were employed in the defence of the Church and her liberties; his strong feelings were poured out towards that Sacred Heart which held up an example of perfect love and suffering; and the proud and passionate nature was quelled and subdued into patience and forbearance, even unto the endurance of death itself, for Christ's sake.

Other saints there have been, perhaps, who have shone more in extraordinary ways and supernatural gifts than S. Thomas of Canterbury; but none, to our idea, has ever more truly embodied the description given by our Lord in the Gospel, of the Good

Shepherd, and which the Church has ordained to be read on his feast:—"I am the Good Shepherd. The good shepherd giveth his life for his sheep. But the hireling, and he that is not the shepherd, whose own the sheep are not, seeth the wolf coming, and leaveth the sheep and flieth: and the wolf catcheth and scattereth the sheep: and the hireling flieth, because he is an hireling and he hath no care for the sheep. I am the Good Shepherd, and I know mine, and mine know Me. As the Father knoweth Me and I know the Father, and I lay down My life for My sheep."—*S. John*, x. 11.

FINIS.

www.ingramcontent.com/pod-product-compliance
Lightning Source LLC
Chambersburg PA
CBHW032152160426
43197CB00008B/879